THE STRUGGLE AGAINST HISTORY

THE STRUGGLE
AGAINST HISTORY

Ronald Segal

WEIDENFELD AND NICOLSON
5 Winsley Street London W1

ISBN 0 297 00451 4

Printed in Great Britain by
Willmer Brothers Limited, Birkenhead

The vanity and presumption of governing beyond the grave, is the most ridiculous and insolent of all tyrannies. Man has no property in man; neither has any generation a property in the generations which are to follow.

Thomas Paine, *Rights of Man*, 1791

CONTENTS

PART I

AN AGE OF REVOLUTIONS

'From what we now see, nothing of reform in
the political world ought to be held
improbable. It is an age of Revolutions, in
which everything may be looked for.'

Thomas Paine, *Rights of Man,* 1791

A spectre is haunting the world – the spectre of revolution. It haunts the corridors of the Kremlin no less than the country clubs of Connecticut and Virginia. It stalks through both Berlins, as through Bengali villages and the banana plantations of Guatemala. It is the upheaval of an affronted humanity, searching for new social relationships. Depending upon who shrinks from its approach, it is democracy, communism, anarchy; and at the same time none of these. For revolution is not generally imminent, or even generally supposed to be so. Paradoxically, the spectre is the more dismaying for being distant, so that its features are indistinct. Indeed, all that may be dimly made out, is that it seems so far different from similar spectres in the past as to provide no guidance to the way it should be confronted. Paradoxically again, a resemblance to such spectres before as materialized in success would be relatively welcome. It would entail an engagement against the known. The age of revolutions that looms is an age with precursors, but essentially without precedent. It would be – and this is the ultimate fear of those who fear it, as it is the ultimate hope of those who hope from it – a thrust into the unknown. It requires, and is exciting, a rejection of much that is in the old revolutionary maps.

For more than a century, these maps were drawn and distributed by those who saw in the working class the sovereign source of social liberation, as they saw in capitalism the inexorably tightening confinement that would supply the impulse. A cartography with the cumulative weight of Marxist analysis behind it, it was founded upon propositions that seemed self-evident enough long after they had first been pronounced. But the character of capitalism has gradually so changed, in a liberal development itself largely influenced by Marxist movements, as to make these propositions correspondingly questionable for the capitalist homelands themselves. Whatever else may have overtaken the conventional working class there, it is patently not destitution. Instead, the techniques of liberal capitalism have afforded a flow of consumer goods so substantial and steady as to consign popular conditions in the great depression of a few decades ago, let alone those in Victorian Britain, to a past almost as alien as the one that upheld the divine right of kings. Vast discrepancies in material living standards still exist, of course; the dynamic of competitive consumption demands no less. Popular poverty must persist, to sustain by contrast the allurement of riches. But it is a poverty different in kind from the poverty of the Marxist proletariat. It is what may be termed relative rather than absolute poverty.

This is not to say that absolute poverty is constant in character across space and time. If hunger has always and everywhere been one criterion, lack of sanitary shelter has, only recently and in countries of advanced industrialization, become another. None the less, such poverty is clearly enough marked in common opinion, at any one time in any one place, for the overwhelming majority on either side to recognize the frontier. And that such poverty exists under liberal capitalism, defies denial. Yet many of those to whom it attaches – the discards of resourceless old age or communal discrimination, of disappearing employment or temperamental disability – are not in work. And others, the seasonal or unskilled labourers in the lowest paid jobs, seem not so much at the bottom of the industrial economy as beyond it. Furthermore, numerous though together they may be, they are still comparatively few. And they seem even fewer: by the different causes of their condition; their residential mobility or diffusion; and their absence of collective commitment. They stand, for society, at its edge.

If these are the destitute of the capitalist momentum, they

are scarcely the proletariat that Marx envisaged. And, to be sure, far from constituting a central working-class challenge of disaffection, they helplessly help to promote a central working-class acquiescence in the system. For their very existence makes relative poverty a sense also of relative advantage, to be accordingly defended. Most workers, caught between fear of where they might fall, and greed for what they might rise to enjoy, have developed the values of liberal capitalism as their own.

The simplification of class antagonism prefigured by Marx has not taken place: because the preconditions of the process have not. Real earnings have not diminished in proportion as the use of machinery and the division of labour have increased. Rather, over extensive areas of industry they have risen so far as to wash away many of the traditional demarcations between working and middle class. Their wages – and commensurate access to credit – provide many skilled workers* with established middle-class standards of consumption: not only in expenditure on the run of obsolescent consumer goods, but also, as with home ownership, in the attainment of lasting, and often appreciating, consumer capital.

At the time that Marx wrote and for long afterwards, the majority of workers in capitalist society were without property beyond a few clothes and the rudiments of furniture. They were and felt themselves accordingly vulnerable. Today they have possessions which represent a sort of material ascendancy over their environment. It is the popular car, perhaps above all, that marks the psychical break between the old capitalism and the new, between the society of class struggle and the society of class accommodation. The car conveys a particular sense of power: not only as a symbol, indeed, but as an object in itself. Driving a car, a man may well feel himself master of his circumstances. He is the generic equal of all those driving; however more elaborate and costly the makes of their cars. He is more powerful, more liberated, at that moment, than the man on the bus or in the train; more powerful, more liberated at that moment than the millionaire on his feet crossing the road. And other consumer goods, if not in quite the same way, provide this impression of power. Clothes are less and less distinctive of social inferiority:

*In iron and steel production, for instance; in the engineering and chemical industries; in certain sectors of power and transport.

3

more and more people can afford to dress with obvious style and expense in seeking the admiration of others. Television sets provide at a turn of the switch not merely an entertainment uniform for rich and poor, but a sense of command, in the very decision of what to see. Every act of consumer choice, in contrast to the necessities of primitive survival, is an experience of power. And the whole process of modern merchandizing astutely encourages and exploits this experience.

What the industrial society of liberal capitalism has accomplished is a blurring of the difference between two distinct kinds of property: consumer and productive. It was a difference which scarcely existed in the days of Marx and for many decades afterwards: because those who possessed the one kind possessed the other; while those who were without, were without both. The majority of workers have not acquired productive property, the property of social power. They have acquired consumer property, the property of material power that is the illusion of social power. And because they acquire more and more of it as the prosperity of mass production mounts, they are partly persuaded that the equality of people is being demonstrated; that the inequality of property is of diminishing importance; and that in so far as they command inferior resources, they also escape the pressures and risks of superior responsibility.

Moreover, if the attainment of productive property through equity purchases is nowhere near as common as the apologists of liberal capitalism pretend, the practice pursued by individual companies, of wooing the allegiance of labour through the bonus distribution or assisted sale of their own shares to their own workers, is likely to spread, with encouragement from government. It is a practice which, by the nature of the system informing it, will scarcely produce the classless commonwealth: but which may well further blur the lineaments of traditional class distinctions.

This class blurring occurs at least as strongly among women as among men. Labour-saving devices in the home; compulsory free schooling of a sort for their children; the use of easy contraceptive methods: such factors have allowed growing numbers of workers' wives to meet their middle-class counterparts in choice; of leisure, or independent earning to raise the family level of consumption. And if increasingly the choice seems an

4

arid one – between the dreariness of employment and the dreariness of leisure – this is a manifestation of the social system that cuts across rather than along conventional class lines. Indeed, to the degree that wives seem increasingly stirred by some common discontent, this derives from the generic relations between men and women in society: and far from fostering among women cohesions of economic class, fosters a cohesive concern with the character of sexual class instead.

Certainly, working conditions themselves have become in general steadily not more, but less repulsive. The achievement of universal adult suffrage, and of government by political parties ostensibly representing the interests of labour; trade unionism, and the impact of organized labour militancy on the competitive position of individual enterprises and countries; the switch in emphasis by industrial management from production to productivity; the strides in technology, with the development of automation and a multitude of new industries: all this has transformed the working environment. The dingy clutter of the old sweat-shop is as far from the modern factory floor, especially in countries with high rates of new industrial investment, like the Netherlands and West Germany, as are the old industrial clashes from the corporate manoeuvres of labour and management today. Steadily, too, the working day, the working week, the working year, the working span is being reduced, alongside increases in total earnings and inducements to early retirement: as the system seeks to promote at once its own material efficiency and popular acceptance of its purposes.

It is true that the repetitive work mainly required by the current techniques of mass production, supplies small source of psychical development. But it is to be doubted whether many established middle-class forms of employment much further extend the reach of the personality. Under its distinctive disguise, the job of the stockbroker or the bathtub manufacturer is scarcely less confined and confining than the job of the welder on an assembly line. The ultimate repulsiveness of most work, as a bondage to be day after day endured, for the escape into the bondage of consumption that it provides, is more and more revealing itself as an inclusively social, rather than an exclusively class, attribute. As the economic possibilities of advanced industrialization make such waste of humanity appear less and less rational, the appeal of work that would stretch instead of stunting the personality, must further displace class antagonisms within the system, by the antagonism of the person to the system itself.

Nor is instability of employment and income, for classic Marxism a crucial factor in the developing self-consciousness and dissaffection of the working class, any longer a valid assumption of capitalist failure. Wages do not, with feverish competition among the bourgeois themselves, dangerously fluctuate; and the demand for labour does not diminish with the mounting introduction and improvement of machinery. On the contrary: industrial wages have securely, if differentially, risen: and advances in mechanization have usually produced labour shortages rather than gluts. This is not to say that the liberal capitalist economy is regular in growth, or has eradicated unemployment. The competition among individual countries within the system produces sporadic retrenchment measures by the less successful. But more often than not, minority racial, or migrant foreign labour communities, and the unskilled always on the margin of employment, suffer disproportionately the consequences. And, in any event, nowhere under liberal capitalism – since it shook off the depression, and found its feet, with the Second World War – has a retrenchment anywhere serious enough to be confused with the slump of Marxist analysis occurred; or unemployment ever reached a properly critical level of the working mainstream.*

The prosperity of the system may be ascribed to several features that have become the commonplace of its reasoning, if not always of its rhetoric. The state has intervened to regulate the temperature of capitalism: by manipulating credit costs and

---

*In the United States, for instance, unemployment was 24.9 per cent in 1933; 17.2 per cent as late as 1939; and 9.9 per cent in 1941. Since then, rates have moved between a low of 1.2 per cent in 1944 and a high of 6.8 per cent in 1958. But any figure above four per cent or so has come to be considered politically untenable. And the Nixon administration moved swiftly in late 1970 to abandon the priority of reducing inflation for the priority of reducing the unemployment rate, to the supposedly acceptable four per cent, by the presidential election of November 1972. The advanced economies of Western Europe have in general, since the Second World War, registered much lower rates than the American: with some like those of Sweden, West Germany, Switzerland, supplementing virtually full employment of the indigenous labour supply with large numbers of foreign workers.

the money supply; management and labour relations; private consumption and public expenditure. And measures of public welfare, from pensions to unemployment and sickness benefits, have blunted the menace of age or other misfortune for the mass of workers. The trade unions provide their members with a sense of protection against outrage by capital, while having themselves been assimilated into the system's efficient functioning. Under the careful charge of bureaucrats, who exercise an established influence on the processes of social decision, they are no mean factor in maintaining a mood of fundamental security.

The increasing dominance of the major corporations, themselves controlled by a bureaucratic compound of the aggressive and the cautious, has substituted monopoly discipline for rugged individualism. Through interlocking directorates, agreements of varying implicitness on price and supply, and cumulative astuteness at fostering profit without too far affronting organized labour or the electoral interests of government, these have significantly reduced the force of competition while perpetuating many of the forms. Alongside the state, they rely more and more upon central planning: investing enormous resources in research, and balancing risks with returns on a scale of years and even decades. And a devotion to deliberate waste has enabled the system to cope with the very abundance of wealth that it creates. The private consumption of agitated covetousness has combined with the massive public expenditure on armaments to squander the surplus that capitalism generates and is essentially unable to use for the collective benefit. What Marx diagnosed as the epidemic of overproduction has so far been sufficiently controlled.

Advances in the application of machinery and in the division of labour have, moreover, proliferated rather than obliterated barriers within the working force itself: raising numerous, often meticulous differences of status and income in and between various types of employment; and producing, far from a dynamic cohesion, a fundamentally centrifugal momentum. If class involves a subjective acknowledgement of association, let alone of common commitment, then where does it today contain together waiters and foundrymen, shop assistants and electricians, bus drivers and computer operators? It seems to separate even the worker who handles complex machinery in the production

7

process, from the worker who sorts through the files in the office of the same factory. Indeed, attempts by the management of certain enterprises in Sweden, for instance, to provide a single canteen for clerical and manual labour have been thwarted by the hostility of the workers themselves to any such integration. In West Germany, many workers are insulted by the suggestion that they belong to the working class; and place themselves determinedly in some indeterminate middle class instead. In Britain, trade unions busily poach members from one another; threaten, take or connive at industrial action to protect the occupational preserves of their own workers against encroachment by others; or merge to swell their particular importance. And meanwhile militancy flares briefly, from one branch, or twig, of employment to another, as wage and status demands are negotiated; and as newly assertive groups of workers, from draftsmen and tax inspectors to aircraft pilots and television technicians, test their distinctive material value to their immediate employers and the social order at large.

If class is ultimately a measure of economic function, then many in employment under liberal capitalism have affiliations so mingled, so ambiguous, as to defy any traditional definition. At what stage do those in the management of substantial enterprises cease to be supervisory labour and become bourgeois? At what stage does share ownership constitute no more than the attempted conciliation of those who remain workers; and at what stage, entrance for them into the class of productive capital? Are trade union bureaucrats, controlling the investment of much accumulated capital but possessing little if any themselves, to be considered members of the working class or of the bourgeoisie? If a man moves from the one to the other only at the precise moment that his capital yields more in disposable income than does his labour, then many of those who manage major private enterprises would have to be classified as workers. And how ought one to classify the top executive of a state enterprise, who may have no productive capital at all but enjoys an annual income from his work that only a very few *rentiers* would find unenviable? Increasingly, through taxation differentials and expense account allowances, governments are favouring the incentives of management over those of simple proprietorship; earned, over unearned income.*

The same social skills afford widely different economic functions. It may well be, for instance, as Marx himself pronounced, that the bourgeoisie has robbed of their haloes professions such as medicine and law and science. But if the inference by Marx, that the doctor, the lawyer, the scientist, would become mere wage labourers of the bourgeoisie, has not been confirmed; neither has its negative. There are, under liberal capitalism, doctors and lawyers and scientists who are as exploited for material profit in their particular employment, as are any assembly-line operatives. But there are others, too, who do the exploiting themselves; who have turned their professions into flourishing commercial or industrial enterprises.

This is not to suggest that the system has surmounted all the serious challenges to its successful survival. Indeed, in the very process of defeating the old, it has provoked new ones, finally more formidable, in their stead. What it does suggest is that liberal capitalist society, by the manipulated excitement of competitive yet popularly rising consumption, has made of classic class struggle little more than folklore. Even in France and Italy, where powerful communist parties command the main trade unions and the bulk of worker votes; and where labour unrest has recently been more massive than elsewhere within the system; class struggle persists in rhetoric far more than in reality. There, as in other countries under liberal capitalism, manifestly most workers are concerned not to alter their collective situation, or the essential priorities of the system itself, but only to raise the immediate return which the system concedes to their respective situations. And their established spokesmen, in party and trade unions, are generally still less allured than they are themselves by revolutionary endeavour: which might fail and produce an expensive repression; or succeed and sweep away the bureaucrats along with the bourgeois. More and more, these do not even pretend to the existence of class struggle any longer. They proclaim labour to be the partner of capital, and themselves

*Though relatively low rates of capital gains tax permit the heavy-weights of capital, with the aid of their professional advisers, to continue, much as T. S. Eliot's hippopotamus, sleeping and feeding at once.

co-directors with the principal proprietors and managers, in a commitment to advance national prosperity and prevalent standards of consumption.*

Certainly, nowhere within the system are the majority of workers really concerned to mitigate – let alone eliminate – the inequalities within the labour force. On the contrary: whether through wildcat strike committees on the shop-floor or the entrenched trade unions, individual groups of workers press their claims to better wages or other conditions of employment: with a hearty disregard in practice, if not always in posture, for the claims of supposed class comrades more poorly placed already than they are. The arena of capital, with the self-promoting superiorities of skill and scale, is mirrored in the arena of labour. If, in recent years, the gap between the higher and the lower-paid has not stayed the same, it has more often widened than narrowed.

It is difficult not to conclude that, with the liberal development of capitalism, the working class, in any such cohesive sense as might promise a Marxist insurgency, has become an anachronism. The mass of workers are, to themselves as to the system which enfolds them in its values, primarily individual consumers. And to the degree that they do recognize a collective identity, it is, paradoxically for the Marxist prognosis, the collective identity of the nation and the race. Time and again they have shown themselves far more responsive to the exclusive invocations of patriotism than to the international solidarity of the exploited; as time and again they have shown themselves fearful and resentful of apparent competition from immigrant or foreign migrant labour. In Britain and the United States, where significant racial minorities exist, workers from the racial mainstream have significantly rallied to the cause of racial discrimination. They care much less that there are those hazily above them than that there should be those distinctly below

---

*In West Germany, the trade unions own and operate the fourth largest bank, along with insurance, housing construction, and other companies: and their ideologues discourse on the policing role of such activity, which ensures competition in capitalism. In Sweden, the trade unions own and operate, among much else, major insurance and building concerns: and their ideologues discourse on the need to nationalize not capital, but the crucial functions of capital, through the appropriate control of credit. In Britain, the trade unions invest in equities: and their ideologues discourse on the advantages to be gained from exploiting the mixed economy.

them. And this is at least as effective in a world, as in the national, context.

Workers under liberal capitalism know that, however poor they may be beside the rich in their respective countries, they are themselves rich beside the mass of humanity. And for most of them, the increasingly troublesome poor of the world, so alien in culture and colour, are accordingly not allies, real or potential, in a conflict with capital: they are threats, real or potential, to the survival of obvious privilege. The parallel with South Africa should not be strained. But there, strikingly, white workers have reconciled themselves to the wide gap between their own living standards and those of the white bourgeoisie, in their devotion to the wide gap between their own living standards and those of the black proletariat and peasantry. Indeed, the South African white bourgeoisie is, in the main, relatively liberal: willing, even eager to discard many racist refinements, in the interests of profitably developing the domestic market and the supply of exploitable skills. But it has been frustrated in this by the demand, to preserve or advance the prerogatives of their colour, from the bulk of white workers.

And not least in dissuading workers under liberal capitalism from a Marxist disaffection, has been the subsequent career of such professingly Marxist insurgency as seems to have succeeded. This effectively means the Russian revolution of 1917. For the Chinese revolution, which alone might properly compete in significance, has involved an overwhelmingly peasant society, culturally and racially remote. It appears to most workers in the West today as correspondingly irrelevant; when not, by its declarations of passion for a revolutionary mankind, correspondingly dangerous. The Soviet Union, on the other hand, projects itself as culturally and racially far closer to the workers of the West. Its regime long dictated the policies and conduct of their communist parties, whose ideological fealty it still enjoys: if not so surely and ubiquitously as before. And it stirs, with its material power second only to that of the United States, all too clear an appreciation of its relevance. It remains the prototype of the Marxist revolutionary state for most workers under liberal capitalism; and a crucial influence, therefore, on their attitudes to such revolution.

Yet what encouragement does the Soviet Union constitute to

11

Marxist commitment and endeavour in the West? Far from weakening nationalist preoccupations, in the cause of the revolutionary struggle by labour everywhere, it has fortified them: as the homeland of socialism has more and more revealed itself to be the vindication of Mother Russia. And unavoidably in promoting its own, it has offended the nationalism of others. The sustenance of bureaucratic regimes in Eastern Europe by the threat or employment of Soviet military might, has done as little to recommend Soviet-style territorial, as to enhance the appeal of Soviet-style popular, sovereignty. And Soviet socialism in the metropolis is hardly more alluring than are its colonial variants. Elections, conducted without public criticism of policy or leaders, and which produce virtually unanimous votes of approval; the show trials of dissident intellectuals; the crude and pervasive censorship of information and ideas; the existence of various elites with lofty standards of consumption: such certainly does not constitute an irresistible democratic contrast to the snap, crackle and pop of packaged politics in the West. Of course, Western mass communications, in private capitalist ownership or controlled by public corporations of capitalist allegiance, make the most of the evidence for intransigent totalitarianism that the Soviet system provides. But who may reasonably doubt that the Soviet system itself provides more than enough evidence?

And in contrast to the years before liberal capitalism found its stride, this evidence is not contradicted, explained or excused by a considerable body of intellectual opinion in the West. On the contrary: the intellectuals of social disaffection there today are far more often to be found condemning than defending the character of the Soviet system. To the degree that they are attracted to any established professingly Marxist regime, it is to one, like the Cuban or Chinese, which seems to represent the insurgency of the world's poor, and to have revealed a sufficient concern with social experiment. The front-line Western apologists for the Soviet system are in the bureaucracies of the communist parties and such trade unions as these control: themselves under increasing attack, for their cynical collaboration with capitalism, from intellectuals of a revolutionary commitment.

Furthermore, the Soviet regime, whatever its ceremonial obeisances to the future of Marxism in the West, is very far from seeking to foment there a Marxist insurgency for affiliation to the Soviet system. It realizes how futile such an exercise would be. But it is, in any event, plainly committed to prosperity in the nuclear age by some form of international condominiun with the United States. In the same way that it would regard as a summons to war or submission the capture by the United States of a country inside the Soviet system, it supposes that the United States would regard the capture, however indirectly achieved, by the Soviet Union of a country inside the system of liberal capitalism.

Countries outside either system, but subject to the protection of one or the other, are a different matter. There contest may be pursued – must be pursued, as a manifestation of what distinguishes the two systems – by a complex set of rules, continually tested and in consequence adjusted. But France and Italy, for instance, with their important communist parties, are none the less seen by the Soviet Union to be as inviolably beyond its grasp, as it expects the United States to see Hungary and Czechoslovakia inviolably within it.*

Each suzerain power has come to accept and respect the other's delimitation of vital interests. And in the process, the Soviet regime has more and more appeared an imperial bureaucracy: concerned abroad, as at home, less with risk and change than with reassurance and stability; not with people, but with the state. Had there been any serious remaining doubt of this before, the strident Sino-Soviet dispute that has so divided

---

*Even before the nuclear pressures of accommodation, indeed, and when the prospect of success for communist party revolt in Western Europe was much more considerable than it is today, the Soviet regime placed first what it saw as the interest of the Soviet state. Thus, towards the close of the Second World War, the armed resistance groups under communist control in France and Italy, were compelled by their respective party leaderships, under orders from Moscow, to approve their own dissolution.

'There is nothing . . . to support the view that the Communist Party seriously gave thought at this time to seizing power even though power was in its reach in various parts of the country. If the Soviet Union meddled at all in French affairs, it was to push the Communists into supporting a government that they did not dominate but that Russia thought they could force to carry out a policy friendly to her. It was exactly the way in which the Soviet Union had operated a few months earlier in Italy . . . Virtually everywhere in Western Europe, for that matter, the Communists forgot the traditional slogan of refusing to collaborate with 'the class enemy' and joined governments led by 'bourgeois' parties for which in the past they had never had strong enough abuse . . . there was the solid determination to have [Soviet] hands free in the east in exchange for such concessions.' André Fontaine, *History of the Cold War*, Secker and Warburg, London, 1968, pp. 197–8.

13

the world communist movement, over the priority of peaceful coexistence or wars of liberation, should surely by now have resolved it.

Above all, Soviet society has long ceased to present a humanist alternative in either substance or intent. It has chosen to compete with liberal capitalism, indeed, on the very terms that liberal capitalism has made its own: joy through material consumption and progress through differentials of power, under the ultimate dominance of property. That productive property is largely state-owned in the one system and largely under private ownership in the other, makes for a distinction of means. But the end is the same. People exist, in both, not to use, but to serve property.

Marx described bourgeois society as one in which capital is independent and has individuality, while the person has no individuality and is dependent; in which the past holds sway over the present rather then the present sway over the past. This is undeniably true of liberal capitalist society, with its merchandising of personal identity and its self-promoting discrepancies in economic and intellectual resources. But is it any less true of a Soviet system which so subordinates the person to the capitalism of the state, and which finds in its avowed corporate achievements, from its universities and its hospitals to its department stores and missile armoury, only a further vindication for keeping social relationships locked up in the bureaucratic drawers of an old captivity?

While the two systems competitively pursue the development of their material technology, neither seems capable of developing ideas or institutions to reorganize society on more creative moral lines. And since the workers under liberal capitalism can descry neither ideas nor institutions in the Soviet system to concentrate their discontents with those in their own, most of them are reduced to mere material comparisons.

They need no distortions of propaganda to realize that in general their standards of consumption are superior. There are simply, today, more motor cars and home appliances, more shades of lipstick and styles of dress for popular enjoyment under liberal capitalism. And the argument from industrial growth rates, the promise of tomorrow's jam, provides liberal capitalism with the post-war star performances of Japan and West Germany. There is, in short, no reason that they can recognize why workers under liberal capitalism should seek to overthrow their own system for the sake of putting the Soviet one in its place.

And yet, an end to the credibility of proletarian revolution in the West is the beginning of a credible popular revolution. For the very failing of faith in the revolutionary commitment of the working class is making room for the growth of a revolutionary commitment unmildewed by illusion. The real predicament of Western society thus revealed lies in the disintegration of the moral consensus which has informed the rise and rule of capitalism: with mounting pressure for a revolutionary alternative, especially from among the young; mounting demands for a rigorously repressive response, to prevent such a future by abandoning the present for the past; and a dominant bourgeoisie of mounting self-doubt and distraction. And, in this process, the present role of organized labour, while apparently the most stabilizing element in the system, is actually most responsible for promoting the system's instability, by requiring that the system remains as it is.

What is fundamentally in operation may, with due deference to Marx and to the crucial role of economic relationships, be termed dialectical idealism. A social system is safe for as long as the people within it sufficiently accept its moral basis: because it seems to serve, at least better than any perceptible alternative, what they have come to consider their paramount human purposes. But, as the system develops, it necessarily reveals its contradictions and inadequacies: provoking a revision of these purposes, and of the proper means by which such purposes may be served. The moral thesis of the system feeds by its very realization the cause of its antithesis; and there follows accordingly a social conflict which can only be resolved by the establishment of a new system instead.

The moral basis of feudalism, for instance, lay in the hierarchical principles of church and state, with the paramount human purposes of piety, justice and order, assumed to be best served by each man's performing the obligations of his particular place. To be sure, the hierarchies of this world did not convincingly correspond to the hierarchies of good and evil in the next. But then human arrangements could no more be perfect than man himself be free of inherent sin. They merely confined the propensity to evil and encouraged the pursuit of good by the disciplines of demarcated duty: relying upon, as they reflected, the ultimate concern with the requitals of the Christian after-life. It was an idealism, like that of the caste system in India, rooted in the essentially static agricultural experience. It was a coming to moral terms with the unyielding natural environment: the captivity of a bare subsistence, punctuated by the calamities of pestilence, famine and war.

Inevitably, however, the system generated the challenge to itself. Its social organization produced economic surpluses which supported the development of trade, free commercial towns, and the importance of money. Trade and its technology in turn promoted the production of, and the impulse to producing, a surplus. New instruments of power thrust against the traditional order and its peculiar idealism of acquiescence, represented by the cardinal virtue of humility. And the process was incidentally much hastened by the Black Death, a fourteenth century outbreak of the plague which reduced the population of Europe by between a third and a half; eroded the influence of the church with the demoralizations of both religious frenzy and cynicism; and intensified the economic pressures of an already diminishing serf labour supply.*

Banker, merchant, mercenary, explorer climbed, as they raised, the dominion of prince and state; while the social role of land, with its closer limits to individual enterprise, declined.

Confronting the moral thesis of hierarchy was its antithesis in equality. And the consequent conflict, raging first in the name of God and then increasingly in the name of man, through the Reformation, the English Civil War, the American War of Independence and the French Revolution, was resolved in the triumph of capitalism. The synthesis was rooted in the dynamism of trade and industrialization, of territorial conquest and scientific or technological discovery. It reflected a new belief in

---

*Yet, if incidental, how accidental was the Black Death? The development of trade, within Europe and from Europe to the East, and the growth in the population density of towns, made the arrival of plague, and the virulence of its progress, the more likely at least.

the ready yielding of the natural environment to the endeavours of the individual and the nation. It made of property instead of place the moral thesis, in an idealism of competition whose cardinal virtue was assertiveness. It made of property the means by which the old paramount purposes of justice and order, and the new ones of freedom and progress, were properly to be served. Property spelt liberation from feudal privilege. It opened the source of social power equally to all. By acquiring it through his own exertions and ability, a man might rise from poverty to riches; while even those left behind were not therefore bondsmen but free, to sell their labour where it paid them best, and to buy for their subsistence and comfort where it cost them least. And property was progress, justice and order as well. It provided the incentive and the opportunity for men to explore and exploit natural resources and their own potential. It rewarded the deserving: whose own material gain, after all, was involved in that of the whole society. And its order, related to personal achievement, was firm and yet flexible; the guarantee both of acquisition and the possibility of acquiring.

The system needed still to develop two primary supports: the politics of universal adult suffrage, and the economics of state intervention. If property had to be unequal, limits had to be set to the inequalities, and their impact on social stability. Through their votes, all citizens could enjoy the same chance to command the functioning of government. And government in turn regulated the functioning of the market, to set a floor under poverty and a ceiling upon riches. Yet in realizing itself, the moral thesis of the system was raising the challenge of its antithesis. And we are now at a point in time when the cause of property is being confronted by the cause of personality: to produce a social conflict that only the synthesis of a new system can resolve.

Capitalism in the United States soon came up against the morally feudal institution of slavery* in the South; and its

*The paradox of slavery is that it belongs, in historical sequence, rather to the age of capitalism than to that of feudalism. But the ages long intermingled, as one system gave way before the other. There are unmistakable remnants of feudalism still, in countries of advanced capitalism. For the slave-trader and owner, of

victory in the civil war seemed to promise the start of an era in which race would become socially irrelevant. In the event, white supremacy recovered in the form of racial segregation, not only to flourish throughout the South but to infect every state of the Union. Yet, far from weakening the moral claim of capitalism, this strengthened it: since, for virtually the entire black body of discontent, racism persisted precisely because capitalism itself was not properly being applied.

Indeed, the emerging militant labour movements achieved small recruitment from the black community: in part because they generally practised racial discrimination themselves; but in part also because they sought, or pretended to seek, the overthrow of capitalism. Where a movement of serious social disaffection did emerge to attract a significantly popular black allegiance – in the Universal Negro Improvement Association of Marcus Garvey, during the early 1920s – it was directed not against the capitalist system, but rather towards establishing a separate black counterpart. The collapse of the movement in debt, scandal, Garvey's imprisonment for fraud and subsequent deportation to his native Jamaica, left the black bourgeoisie, which had been overwhelmingly hostile to the Garveyite gospel of racial separatism, in reinforced charge of articulate community opinion. From their base in the churches, in commerce, and in the professions, especially education, its spokesmen continued crying for a consistent capitalism that would lead them to the promised land of racial integration.

The Great Depression, which brought so many whites so much closer to the common experience of most blacks, and the coming of the New Deal with its liberal emphasis on the responsibility of the state for promoting public welfare, seemed to enhance the prospects of success for the integrationist cause within the system. And the acrobatics of the communist party, with black separatism now adopted as the racial solution and

course, the slave himself was no more than a particular form of capital. But in the moral meaning of feudalism, with the inflexible subserviences and prerogatives of place, the institution itself was far more feudal than capitalist, for the society at large. Clearly capitalism, with one of its fundamental moral principles in the freedom of labour, was bound to reject slavery: because the mass of free labourers saw the institution as a threat to their proper survival; while those capitalists employing free labour saw themselves at a disadvantage in competition with those who possessed slaves.

then anathematized again for the exclusive demands of the class struggle, did little to undermine the black commitment to capitalism. American involvement in the Second World War, with the cascade of democratic rhetoric that accompanied it, restored failing integrationist hopes. And if these were scarcely fulfilled, there was sufficient evidence of a change in white public opinion, especially with the cold war contest for coloured allegiance in the world at large, to encourage confidence that the system would now, in its own interests, have genuinely to mend its ways. The Supreme Court in 1954 declared racially segregated schooling unconstitutional: in terms that assailed the long established principle of separate if equal. The civil rights movement, with the increasing engagement of the black churches, and with liberal sympathy stirring the surface of the nation, began confronting the racial rigidities of the South. Boycotts and marches of protest, extracting anxious expressions of support from elected federal authority, made headway fast enough to excite by its slowness the hopeful militancy of the young. An allegiance of black and white students, eschewing violence but challenging directly, with such methods as sit-ins and picket lines, manifestations of racism, even in the centres of comfortable liberalism outside the South, achieved some famous victories.

And then, suddenly, it seemed, the disposition of protest was different. By the time of the Voting Rights Act in the summer of 1965, with its promise of changing at last the structure of political power in the South through the federal enforcement of equal citizen suffrage, rioting had raged through the black ghetto of one city after another; black separatism was disrupting the student alliance; and the overthrow of the system was increasingly informing the language of disaffection, both within the black community and on the campus. But if the new mood seemed sudden, this was because its persistent approach had gone unnoticed.

It was not that liberal capitalism had for so long failed to solve the problem of racism. The perception had developed that the problem was intrinsic to the system. And paradoxically the very success of the constitutional struggle had developed the perception. For the more that the forms of racial equality had been conceded, the more disillusioningly the force had been denied. The federal government might assault the principle of

19

racially segregated residence or education; but the practice was being promoted by the operations of the system itself.

Indeed: so many slums are and stay distinctively black because the blacks in them so commonly are and stay poor; so many suburbs are and stay so distinctively white, because the whites in them so commonly are and stay rich. That this correspondence of race and poverty has its genesis deep in the past is not to be denied; but it is no more to be denied that capitalism carries the discriminations of the past into the future. The poor are less skilled; and, for being poor and less skilled, less confident of their capacity to compete: less skilled and less confident of their capacity to compete, the poor remain poor. The slum and the suburb perpetuate themselves and each other: through their characteristic homes and schools and streets. And this results not from some accidental functioning of capitalism, but from the moral thesis that makes capitalism function as it does.

The truth is that racism belongs not, as so many blacks so loyally for so long believed, to the effective inconsistency of capitalism, but to its effective consistency. How would the inequalities of property survive, were the equality of people really to be pursued? How should capitalism itself continue, without some men being materially deprived so that others might the more abundantly enjoy? It is the nature of the system to exclude rather than to include; to foster preoccupations of above and below. In fact, racial inequalities are an important feature of the American psychical market in failure and success. Whites lower down the scale of competitive consumption can reassure themselves by social processes that rank them higher than blacks. And blacks higher up the scale than many whites can accordingly compensate for their racial drawbacks.

That the traditional leaders of the black community did find such compensation was a powerful prop to capitalism in the United States. But it is a prop now substantially eroded. More and more blacks, especially among the young, in or from a background of business or the professions, are not rejecting the system because they feel themselves materially deprived as individual victims of racism. Rather, for many of them racism has proved privately profitable. The liberal leadership of the system has promoted efforts to counter the mounting resentment of the degraded mass; and business corporations, universities, trade unions, political parties have increasingly preferred, beyond customary definitions of desert, blacks for a display of racial indifference. But this, while doubtless materially agreeable to those so preferred, has swollen rather than drained their psychical discontent. Exceptions that prove the rule are not necessarily more comfortable for being such; and in their very advantages, these blacks descry the disadvantage of their race.

However materially rich some blacks may be, they feel themselves socially poor; as the materially poor mass of blacks feel themselves socially poorer, more deprived, than any whites in similar material circumstances. Even, therefore, were the system to invest far larger a proportion of its material product than it shows credible signs of ever doing, in rescuing the bulk of the black community from the squalors of city ghetto and rural slum, it would not end the tormenting sense of poverty provided by racial disparagement. But then the system is, of course, essentially unwilling to make the material investment, because it is essentially unable to make the moral one. It is this realization, that the system is a blind alley of hope, which has finally fired a significant black revolutionary movement.

To say that this black revolutionary movement is significant, is not, however, to say that it has united the community behind it. The Black Muslims still represent a Garveyite withdrawal into racial separatism, for its own and for its living prophet's sake: employing methods and setting objectives that are more a mimicry than a renunciation of capitalism. The National Association for the Advancement of Colored People (NAACP) has continued to believe in constitutional pressures, through the courts and the electoral contest of the two major parties, as the best way of making the system live up to its moral pretensions. The disciples of Martin Luther King, Jr, mainly in the South, cling yet to the possibility of turning, through non-violent mass action and the Christian appeal, the American nightmare into the dream. Nor is the movement united within itself. There are Black Panthers who treat revolution as something more than racial conflict. But among many other advocates of an insurgent black power – not to speak of those who exploit the call as no more than an electoral slogan – there is a plethora of merely negative commitments.

21

What does seem at present clear is that there are black revolutionaries, resolved and organizing to overthrow the social system; that they are willing to use violence, and are undismayed by the potential consequences to themselves or to others of the black community; that much of the black community is sympathetic enough to provide them with moral and material support and protection; and that the more their representatives appear, as have the Black Panther leaders, hunted by authority, the more recruits they attract from the community. Such, to be sure, does not produce a revolution in the United States. What it has already produced, if not on its own but in concert with other factors, is the social climate of a pre-revolutionary period: a widespread public sense that events are reaching beyond the control of the established order; that the desertions from the system must in time critically confront it; and that the outcome must be as uncertain as the engagement will be costly. And the development of this climate in itself nourishes the revolutionary impulse. Taken seriously by society, the revolutionaries take themselves more seriously as a result, and the more convincingly propagate their cause.

This cause must be informed by an idealism in opposition to that of the system. And the search for a moral antithesis, to counter the thesis of property, is perhaps best to be followed among black Americans in the complex concept of 'soul'. This is, initially, a collective identification, asserting the peculiar nature of black experience and personality. But this peculiarity is one of defeat and denial; of outrage: as well as of resilience and achievement. It becomes a commitment to revolt. 'Soul' means the readiness, of the black people and the black person, to confront the system: for the making of a new one, that will answer the needs and serve the purposes of the black personality. And meaning this, 'soul' means something beyond the peculiarly black assertion. It becomes the assertion of personality itself, against a system whose needs and purposes distort and deprive it. 'Soul' is the cry of individual man, for the equal freedom to enjoy and to extend his individuality: against the unequal subjugations that are the despotism of property.

It is here, properly, in the moral antithesis, that the black meets the other significant revolutionary movement in the United States: among the young and especially the students. The two movements, of course, overlap. The black draws much of its force and leadership from the young, not least the students, of the racial community. And the white revolutionaries owe much to the past of the civil rights struggle; as they do to the example of the present black challenge. Certainly, in the beginnings of their movement, it was their own experience of the system's recalcitrant racism, in their work alongside black student militants, that provoked many to question the system itself and proceed to engage it in other of its repressive manifestations. Students were, and still are, at the centre of this movement. But the causes and course of their particular disaffection must be seen in relationship to that wider phenomenon: the increasing disaffection among the young. And to consider of what this consists involves some scrutiny of how and why it seems to have come about.

Society under liberal capitalism has remained structurally authoritarian, while the traditional sanctions of the structure are constantly being undermined by the functioning of the system itself. The patriarchal family model that so suited the development of capitalism, with the father as the symbol and the substance of the power exercised by propery, has been eroded: by the vast expansion in demand for labour, especially such as is young enough to be trained in new skills, and by the shift in social emphasis from producer to consumer. Women may go out to work and earn for themselves: while if the young may not do so already, they have not long to wait. Meanwhile the market place pays to both a regard in accordance with their dominance of consumption. The culture of consumption itself, with its emphasis on the new, advances the claims of youth rather than age. And on the vital level of myth, the mounting control of the economy, as of politics, by corporate management, is steadily wasting the lonely patriarchal image of hunter, warrior, pioneer, intrepid entrepreneur.*

*Inside the black community, above all in the tumultuous ghettoes, the relatively high incidence of families headed by the female, through broken marriages or illegitimate births or temporarily absent husbands; and the high rate of male unemployment, with the often contrasting availability of jobs, in domestic service or clerical work, for women, have done still more to destroy a patriarchal pattern of authority there.

Sexual sanctions have been assailed by scientific and technological developments. It is not only that women have been given a new independence by the mass production and marketing of simple and reliable contraceptives for their use. But the young have been encouraged, by the existence of such contraceptives, to explore, in sexual experience, a crucial area of personal relationships and responsibility: before these explorations are permitted any counterpart in the superficial processes of social decision. From their relative distance, they are quick to mark the incompatibility of the prevalent priorities with their own moral evaluations.

There has been, too, a manifest decline in the force of the established religious sanctions: nourishing, as it is nourished by, the decline in established secular ones. A society centred on the market place may well be congenial to the cultivation, by contrast, of spiritual disciplines: but scarcely such as are delivered by institutions which have set up stalls themselves and are closely associated with the general management. In short, traditional organized religion seems to have a diminishing appeal for the young: and among those still being drawn or held, there is increasing impatience with the structure and preoccupations of authority. Even within the long obedient ranks of the Roman Catholic devout, recent papal pronouncements reaffirming past attitudes on birth control and on the celibacy of the clergy were openly and widely argued and contradicted. And where the young were themselves not active in the dispute, the impact on their allegiance was an important concern of the disputants.

All this has, of course, to be connected with an upheaval in the order of knowledge. Mass literacy, produced by compulsory schooling and eagerly serviced by the publishing industry, has progressively promoted the circulation of new ideas and doubts among the young. And there has been a development of science and technology so rapid and profound that children acquire in the classroom procedures of learning which mystify their parents, and take for granted concepts at which a previous generation still marvels. The intellectual sanctions of age seem less and less convincing to young and old alike.

Television has played a particularly seditious role. Alongside the most banal entertainment and the psychical assaults of advertising, which treat all age groups with indiscriminate disrespect, it has brought wars and elections, social criticism and conflict, into the home: where censorship of what the young receive is difficult to practise, when practised at all. What emerges of the society that their elders have helped to make, and hopefully or helplessly yet accept, is not such as to foster the respect of the young for the judgement of age. Television has, too – if, so often, despite itself – dispelled some of the ignorance and illusion on which nationalism thrives. It has made the presence of mankind more real and more relevant; as it has made war less romantic, and poverty less remote. And accordingly it has weakened the patriotic sanctions that support the authoritarianism of the state.

All but gone now are the sanctions of the traditional neighbourhood: since the neighbourhood itself has no place in the system's peculiar social mobility. The halls and cafés and bars and shops, the parks and pavements, of a defined community: where people met to talk a while, exchanging their news and their opinions; where proprieties of thought and conduct were passed from one generation to the next: such places serve these functions seldom, if ever, in the incoherent megalopolis. With the social measure of his failure or success so dependent on his address of the moment, the person does not live in a neighbourhood: he lives in a slum, a housing estate, a suburb, a luxury high-rise; in an apartment only a short walking distance away from the most fashionable shops, or one only a short walking distance away from where the ghetto begins; in a street, or on the side of a street, 'going up' or 'going down'. The exclusive concerns of competitive consumption drive out the inclusive ones of community coherence. The paramount relationship of the person to the commodity leaves little time or appetite for the demands of the relationship between people. It becomes easier, and more natural, to communicate with a television set than with a neighbour. And the young have only their own neighbourhood to make, among themselves.

Above all, perhaps, the sanction of traditional realism has been sapped. It is clear that the new implications of total war have been an important element in exciting revolt at the system among those born into the nuclear age. Indeed, for many of the young, the very reasonableness of the realism responsible for the nuclear terror must be doubted. The readiness to risk the annihilation of mankind seems to belong to a system of the supremely unreasonable, which has found its way only to the supremely unreal.

Alongside this erosion of essential sanctions, the system has eroded its essential appeal in material consumption. It is not that the market place has ceased to empty the pockets of the young; but that it has ceased to dominate their minds. The rebel generation spends more on commodities than did any of its predecessors, because it has so much more to spend, and because the system is so adept at meeting any new material demand. The market will provide bead necklaces and head bands, peace buttons and revolutionary texts, as it will provide nerve gas or napalm, for a suitable profit. But the acquisitive appetite is not for the young the force that it was for their fathers. If there are many who still experience material need, as in the black ghettoes, they are increasingly concerned with changing the moral basis of the society that denies them, rather than with striving for the means of instant satisfaction. And they are much outnumbered by those who have known only an immediate environment of material choice. For these last, the distresses of the great depression, remembered so anxiously by their parents, are as distant as the days of the Red Indian displacement: more distant, indeed, since the great depression is not nearly so often the subject of cinema and television romance. To the degree that they are psychically less trapped, they are the more able to consider critically the culture of consumption which encompasses and threatens to overwhelm them.

The system itself, by its corporate functioning and discriminations, feeds this moral insurgency. More and more, the young have come to be treated, and to treat themselves, as a separate class, with its peculiar commitments. Business managers, market researchers, academic experts, reporters and editors, politicians, parents examine and declare what it is that the young desire and demand, resent and resist. Identifying 'life-styles', from fashions in hair to the smoking of pot, are disseminated as they are described, derided, assailed by publicity. Movements and demonstrations of protest and revolt are seized upon by the mass communications industry; and the ideas informing them, spread in the process further and faster than their adherents could sensibly hope ever on their own to achieve. Thus, in the very exploiting of the young as a corporate market and a corporate source of entertainment and news, the system helps them to discover and develop a distinctive disaffection: much as it helped black disaffection to discover and develop itself.

But if the disaffections of the young and of the black are distinctive, they are also the same. For among the young, too, the moral antithesis pursued is that of personality. Different expressions of the pursuit have produced different moral passwords. But containing them all, as 'soul' may be said to contain the cumulative expressions of black search and assertion, has been the concept of 'love'. For it is 'love' that from the start seemed most clearly to propound a creative individual search and assertion, through a society of inclusive personal relationships; as it seemed most clearly to contradict the destructive nature of a system concerned with the exclusive relationships of property. Like 'soul', the concept was essentially, insistently revolutionary. And like 'soul', it came to mean, for more and more of the young, the resolve not just to question and protest; but to confront and destroy the system itself.

This is not to say that all or even most of the young – any more than all or even most of the blacks – are committed to revolution. Nor is it to deny that much of the revolutionary commitment which has developed, remains unorganized beyond specific occasions of conflict with authority. All that may sensibly be maintained is that there exists now a significant revolutionary commitment among the young; that there are those within this commitment ready to use violence against a system which they regard as intrinsically violent; and that, like its counterpart among the blacks, and in association with it, this commitment seems to inform a pre-revolutionary period.

Further, like its black counterpart, the revolutionary commitment among the young is not to be contained in some ideological box of the past. To be sure, there is an Old Left, dedicated to repeating history. But the movement of disaffected idealism belongs in the main to a New Left of distinctive preoccupations and objectives. This owes much to Marxism, of course: if often indirectly, through comment and interpretation; and negatively, also, through a repugnance to what professingly Marxist parties and states have done. And it owes much to the

American strain of insurgent thought, from Roger Williams in the colonial beginnings, through Emerson and Thoreau, to Scott Fitzgerald and Allen Ginsberg. But most important of all, it is what it is through its own experience of the system, and of the engagement it has undertaken. People and events constantly influence the course of the commitment. 'I found myself', one young American describing the progress of his decision to desert from military service in Vietnam, earnestly declared during a television programme. And such may well stand for the revolutionary stirrings among the American young. As individual young Americans are doing, so their collective resistance is finding itself: by being, encountering, becoming.

The phenomenon has its centre among the students, where it first seriously manifested itself, and where it has continued to attract its most numerous recruitment. One explanation lies in the extraordinary cohesion of the campus. The young are there together, in an overwhelming majority; instead of being diffused, as one more minority, through the society at large. Ideas spread, and meetings or demonstrations may be organized, with corresponding ease and speed. And the consequent sense of collective identity, even when unaroused by the promptings of revolt, reacts against the counter-attacks of authority: especially if coming from outside, with the introduction of police or the National Guard. In the Free Speech Movement of 1964, on the University of California's Berkeley campus – the first major engagement in the specifically student conflict with the system – demonstrations of protest and defiance followed always swiftly, and often spontaneously, the events that provoked them. The repressive response of academic authority, and in particular the attempts to isolate and punish the leaders, only advanced the cause of revolt: until some two-thirds of the student body supported the objectives, and about one third the tactics, of the movement. And with the direct intervention of the Californian government, which dispatched police to clear the administration building of a mass student sit-in, campus support for the movement still further increased.*

Nor is the immediate campus the sole site for the developing

*These estimates of support came from independent surveys: accepted as reliable by the Byrne Committee which was itself appointed by the University of California's Board of Regents to investigate the Berkeley troubles.

sense of collective identity which is so involved in the development of student disaffection. The various campuses are
themselves connected: through branches of one or other student
organization, with its co-ordinating officials and organs of
propaganda; and, more profoundly, through the experiences that
students across the society come to share. It was from many
different campuses that students streamed to Mississippi in 1964,
for a summer vacation of civil rights work; and the relationships,
personal and ideological, formed in the process of the project,
prefigured that network of sympathy and communication which
would so much more massively promote, and in turn be
promoted by, the student campaign against the Vietnam War.

And informing all this, has been the peculiar experience of the
system that the university itself affords. The immediate cause of
the Berkeley Free Speech Movement lay in sudden restrictions
on the activity of campus clubs. Student militants had been busy
organizing and demonstrating against racist practices not only in
the remoteness of the deplorable South, but intolerably in
Berkeley's own Bay Area: and the local chieftains of business
and politics had pressed the university authorities into taking
counter-measures. Even clubs of avowed conservative outlook
lent cautious support to the campaign against the new
restrictions, which they saw as infringements of basic student
rights. But the movement's emerging leadership increasingly
concerned itself rather with the subservience of the university
to a repugnant social order. Indeed, the hostility to this subservience was all the more fervent for possessing an element of
disillusionment.

The established liberal command of higher education had
persistently proclaimed the principle of intellectual home rule:
the fundamental function of the university to encourage independent thinking and hence moral criticism. Yet it was
precisely against any significant realization of such independent
thinking and hence moral criticism that the liberal command
reacted, as soon as the security of the social system required it to
do so. What, then, was this academic commitment to the value
of the autonomous mind, but an attempt to conceal the disturbing irrationalities of society behind the display shelves of some
intellectual toy shop for the elite? And once so aroused, student
disaffection probed further, to discover and assail other com-

ponents of the tribute paid by the academic to the social order: in the campus facilities for recruitment to corporate business; in the influence on the direction of university research exercised by private enterprise, through financial grants or the membership of governing boards; in the projects undertaken on behalf of and with funds from the military. As the ghetto seemed to more and more blacks, so the university was becoming for more and more students, an embodiment of the total contradiction between the humanist claims of the system and its actual priorities.

It was a contradiction provocatively apparent in the educational process itself. At Berkeley, with close on thirty thousand of them swamping the capacities of staff and equipment, students all too easily saw themselves seen as only so much raw material: to be sorted, processed and packaged for the market place. Few of them ever even met those who contrived and conducted their courses; and most were under such pressure to achieve an adequate grading, for their delivery from one stage of the production schedule to the next, that they hardly had the advertised opportunity to explore the possibilities of their minds. And presiding over this experience was an administration so intrusive and yet so remote that it seemed to be everywhere and nowhere at once. Its representative impersonality was the IBM computer, several of whose identifying cards each student required. The celebrated poster paraded on the campus during the days of the Free Speech Movement – 'I am a UC student. Please don't bend, fold, spindle or mutilate me' – was the cry of an affronted and insurgent individuality: as the relationship between the particular student revolt and the peculiar disaffection of the young was caught in another slogan that the Free Speech Movement popularized – 'You can't trust anyone over thirty'.

The Vietnam War now momentously promoted the moral disquiet and dissent from which the revolutionary commitment was emerging. The system seemed bent on betraying the essential deception of its democratic forms. Lyndon B. Johnson swept to victory in the 1964 presidential election not least because of the contrast between his own soothing view of how the American role in Vietnam should be enacted, and the hot gospelling of his Republican opponent, Barry Goldwater. Within a few months, North Vietnam was being continually bombed; and within three years, the total of the American forces at war in the South had soared from some 23,000 to half a million. What, then, had the policy differences over Vietnam in the election been all about? And what did it matter that one candidate rather than the other had lost? Especially on the campuses, where student organized teach-ins set out to search and destroy the substance of the government's case, more and more of the young saw the American involvement in Vietnam as sustaining there a regime of privilege against peasant revolution: for the sake of safeguarding the ascendancy, at home and abroad, of a system towards which they themselves felt only a deepening antipathy. And they belonged to the very age group from which conscripts were being drawn to fight such a war. Their antagonism advanced from meetings and marches of constitutional protest to the defiant burning of draft cards and attempts to arrest military traffic. Meanwhile, too, the moral and material investments of the system in the war made it still more evident that nothing effectual would or could be done by the social order to end black estrangement.

Public opinion polls registered a rapid climb in electoral anxiety and doubt. With a multitude of young campaigners, sufficiently undisaffected to believe that the system might yet be rescued from itself, Senator Eugene McCarthy stood on a somewhat uncertain peace platform in the New Hampshire Democratic primary for the presidential nomination. He polled unexpectedly well, and Johnson soon afterwards announced his retirement from the race. But at the Democratic nominating convention of August 1968 in Chicago, the results of such primary contests were overwhelmed by the support for Vice-President Hubert H. Humphrey, from the operatives of the party machine and their constituency in the corporate entrenchments of capital, labour and the ethnic minorities.

In the streets outside, the Chicago police went on the rampage, against young demonstrators and anyone else happening to be in reach: with a brutality at which the Democratic leadership cautiously connived, and which seemed to confirm the cry of the revolutionary commitment that the system itself was irredeemably

31

repressive. And meanwhile a rebuff had been given to residual black faith in the system. With hopes which owed rather more to the skills of merchandising than to the quality of the product, there remained a substantial market in black America for the Kennedy determination to confront poverty and racism. But Senator Robert Kennedy was assassinated at the close of his campaign to win the California primary. Just who assassinated him, and why – as who had assassinated Martin Luther King, Jr, and why, a few weeks before – was far less important than what the assassinations themselves seemed to declare: that the very prophets of racial reconciliation within the system fell victims to the system's functioning.

In the event, Richard Nixon, as the Republican nominee, won the presidential election: in a contest which, for all its electronic equipment, was musty with the past. He had campaigned principally on the need to secure law and order and on the promise of somehow, with national power and prestige undebased, winding up the American involvement in the Vietnam War. When, in April 1970, he ordered American forces openly into Cambodia, campuses across the United States erupted in protest of a new magnitude. And, significantly, the immediate climax occurred not at one of the major East or West Coast universities with a record of turbulence, but at Kent State University, Ohio. There, in white middle America, among a youth overwhelmingly from the homes of Nixon's solicited 'silent majority', demonstrators burned the campus quarters of the officer training programme; and troops of the National Guard, dispatched by the Governor to quell the continuing disorder, opened fire and killed four students.

Significantly, too, the first mass demonstration in support of the government and its policies came from building workers gathered in Wall Street, at the scene of a plunging stock market. Indeed, as stock prices tumbled, from Zurich to Tokyo, in the wake of New York, even the usual exuberance of financial journalism gave way to suggestions that there were clouds over the face of capitalism itself. For if the system were to succumb in the United States, the prospects of its survival elsewhere were not encouraging. And clearly, in the United States, it was in more than merely technical difficulties. These the system had proved often enough in the past adept at meeting with successful readjustments. And what such readjustments could achieve, the system would doubtless speedily discover. But now there were, louring through the silver linings, the signs of an approaching social crisis.

The Vietnam War and other American military engagements to the security of the system, including the insatiable demands of ultimate dominance in the technology of destruction; the competitive thrusts of skilled industrial workers towards higher standards of living, and the new militancy of others, like public employees, at being outpaced; the essential impulse of business to ever greater private profit; the increasing costs of providing an electorally acceptable level of public welfare: all combined to promote a rate of inflation which the vigour of trading rivals and the impact on important sectors of domestic opinion made manifestly unsafe. And, indeed, the deepening belief that such inflation had become endemic, inescapable, was itself feeding the disease. Yet what cure could be found within the limited laboratory of the system?

A cut in public expenditure would come at precisely the time when an enormous rise was required: to save public education from self-accelerating decay, and the cities from cumulative neglect; to arrest, let alone reverse, the physical and psychical momentum of poverty, above all in the racial ghetto; to bring some social efficiency into the mounting confusion of transport; and at last, since it had become a political issue of moment, to start dealing credibly with the persistent pollution of the environment. Tight money policies would lower the level of business activity; but in doing so, would lower as well the tax revenues for public expenditure.* And they threatened to produce a measure of unemployment politically untenable if not socially explosive. Besides, the rule that economic retrenchment blunted the militancy of industrial workers with rising unemployment seemed to have been forgotten by such workers themselves.

But then the difficulties of the American social order were not unique. They reflected the difficulties in which the system was almost everywhere finding itself.† Labour was increasingly ex-

---

*The mounting deficits of American budgeting were making other countries in the system more and more anxious over their huge and swelling dollar reserves.

†If Japan seemed something of a notable exception, it was because the system there was largely less developed, and able still to profit from an earlier cultural

ploring and exploiting its bargaining strengths in the market place: as the experience of the great depression, of the Second World War, and of the impulse to national economic recovery, receded, or belonged for the young to an unrememberable past. Example itself was the most stirring of agitators. The surrender of substantial wage rises to workers in the industrial vanguard of products and profits, or otherwise pivotally placed in the economy, excited in those behind them efforts to catch up, or at least to restore the previous distance between.

Such new militancy might not in general challenge the dominion of the system. But this presupposed that the system would continue to reward allegiance sufficiently; and the definition of 'sufficiently' climbed as if reached. Even in Sweden and West Germany, worker unrest was spoiling the proud record of industrial accommodation. The bureaucracies of organized labour were losing command; and the decision to strike or accept the offerings of management increasingly came from the shop-floor. France in the spring of 1968 had proved how massively worker discontent could burst through the safeguards of trade union enmeshment in the system; and Italy was not far behind.

Yet the system could scarcely thrive by conciliating militant labour at the expense of satisfying the overall social demand for public services and welfare, from roads and schools and hospitals to pensions and unemployment benefits. Such was the very basis of manipulative politics: the electoral spine of liberal capitalism. And leaving aside all considerations of the impact on relations among states within the Western power bloc; between the Western and the Soviet power blocs; and between the West and the world of the increasingly troublesome poor: military expenditure could not be seriously reduced without serious injury to influential sectors of capital and labour,* and to intrinsic methods of overall economic management.

mentality. But it needed a powerful faith in collective Japanese idiosyncrasy to believe that corporate business would much longer clip the coupons of paternalism; or that the comparative neglect of public services, and certainly the comparative advancement of environmental pollution, would much longer elude a political reckoning. Surely, however peculiar the process might be in Japan, the development of the system to its essential crisis would be no more evadable there than anywhere else. And in the meantime, of course, the industrial advantages accruing to the country's social lag, looked likely to increase rather than diminish the difficulties confronting competitors in trade.

*A cut-back in defence and related space race expenditure in the United States

Least of all, could capital itself be denied its duly rising expectations of profit. For inseparable from the development of the system was the mounting mobility of money, with its mounting immunity to effective territorial control. Huge multi-national corporations, such as those in the oil industry, in chemicals and electronics, in motor car manufacturing, could all too clearly affect the career of government by switching their liquid holdings from one national currency to another, or by cutting plans for expansion in a particular country until the climate for capital there became more congenial. And all too quickly, the alarm of numerous individual citizens, from those with important business contacts abroad, to those with no more opportunity than their suitcases allowed, could be translated into a flood of funds across the borders: to drain national savings and currency reserves. Capital might attempt to restrain the material aspirations of labour by calls to the cause of country; but it saw no reason why it should disparage the sacrifices of labour by sharing in them.

The crucial truth is that liberal capitalism cannot generate the resources, material and moral, which it conditions society to demand. And in consequence it survives increasingly by deceit: by an increasingly perilous process of material and moral inflation.

By its competitive dynamic, and the effect of this on both the extent and the distribution of the social product, the system does not, and cannot, satisfy the material desires that it excites. And since it does not, and cannot, supply sufficient of the substance, to satisfy at least such socially expressed desires as it dare not deny, it makes up the difference with shadow: by money that pretends to buy more than it will. But the more that shadow has to be supplied in place of substance, the more allowance is made for shadow in the social expression of desires, and the more shadow yet must be supplied to continue making up the difference. The process has not, so far, been precipitate. But it has been in-

---

soon produced the sort of unemployment that was politically unacceptable in the system. Jobless Ph.Ds, it was soon enough remarked, made a more menacing social noise than did an equivalent number of jobless other workers.

exorable; and, however irregular, finally progressive. Well orchestrated incomes policies, with government guidelines or regulations for the restraint of wages and prices; credit squeezes and juggling with the money supply at a necessary distance from the next elections: such attempts to slow down the momentum have more often than not ended in accelerating it.

And inevitably informing this momentum of material inflation, is the momentum of the moral one. The system does not, and cannot, satisfy the moral desires that it excites. It does not, and cannot, provide the personal freedom, and the equality of opportunity; the compassion and security; the experience of extended individuality, that it claims. And since it does not, and cannot, supply sufficient of the substance, to satisfy at least such socially expressed desires as it dare not deny, it makes up the difference with shadow: by a vocabulary – of purposes, priorities, assurances – that pretends to mean more than it will. But here, too, the more that shadow has to be supplied in place of substance, the more allowance is made for shadow in the social expression of these desires, and the more shadow yet must be supplied to continue making up the difference. The moral, as the material, currency further and faster depreciates; promoting a disintegration of the social consensus without which the system cannot stand.

But the disaffected response to this inflationary momentum is far from being monopolized by the revolutionary commitment, or the cause of the moral antitheses. There is, also, in the disintegrating of the social consensus, the disaffected response of the counter-revolutionary commitment: or what may be termed the cause of the prototypal thesis. For the adherents of this, the moral and material inflationary momentum is a sign not of capitalism's intrinsic progress, but of its extrinsic corruption. And they demand an abandonment of the present not for some future of social experiment, based on freedom rather than on order, and on personality rather than on property; but for a return to a past of social certainty, based on the realization of freedom through order, and of personality through property, when the moral and the material currency of the system was alike true to its bond.

36

That this past never existed; that even if it had existed, it could not be recaptured; and that even if it could be recaptured, it would number almost all of those who sigh or clamour for it, among the victims: such has no place in their blend of anxious nostalgia and affronted idealism. The past is simply a panacea by contrast with the present; and to regain it, by restoring capitalism to the purity of its promise, is to surmount the perplexity of problems that beset their lives. It is, in the United States, to re-establish the respect of youth for age, of black for white, of citizens for country; the proper rewards of initiative and hard work, with the proper retributions of indolence and fecklessness; peace from protest and riot and crime in the streets at home, and peace through unassailable power abroad. It is to re-enjoy a sense of neighbourliness and social cohesion, with the susceptibility of government to personal contact and pressure; a physical environment of safe and tidy and tranquil prosperity; the era of golden occasion for the individual, in the confidence of a benevolent future, more or less under the guardianship of God.

To recite the irrationalities of the counter-revolutionary commitment is not, however, to dismiss the commitment as unimportant. The system itself is irrational enough; and it is scarcely wonderful that it should promote a powerfully irrational reaction. Indeed, as the social consensus disintegrates, the revolutionary commitment must itself foster support for the counter-revolutionary alternative. And the evidence suggests that initial success is far more likely for the second than for the first. Certainly the social sources, real and potential, for the pursuit of the prototypal thesis seem immediately far more formidable.

Reacting primarily to the moral inflation of the system, are some of the rich, especially those who made their fortunes rapidly or recently. Helped rather than hurt by material inflation, they are preoccupied by the persistent fall in the purchasing power of the moral dollar, which seems the more to remove from them, the more it offers, a social authority commensurate with their material achievement. They are, whether in oil or real estate, manufacturing or medicine, essentially individual entre-preneurs, who feel themselves shut out from the major processes

37

of social decision and in increasing danger from the increasingly corporate functioning of the system. Paradoxically, therefore, though they have profited so under the regime of big government and big corporate business, it is precisely big government and big corporate business against which they level much of their rage. It is these that they hold largely responsible for the insidious corruption of capitalism: with the feebleness, if not the considered treachery, of the reply to communism at home and abroad; the surrender to blackmail from trade unions and other predatory pressure groups; the indulgence of irresponsible students and insatiable blacks; the encouragement of crime and violence through judicial mollycoddling; the breakdown of order and respect. If order and respect are, indeed, their moral watchwords, it is because they are uncertain of their rightful place in the one and their rightful command of the other. Their hostility to the 'impudent snobs'* of the liberal establishment with its old money and practised authority, as to the 'egg-heads' or intellectuals, is a denial and assertion at once of what they see as their peculiar weaknesses.

On their own, to be sure, they are of minor moment. Their numbers are necessarily small. Their significance lies in the articulate leadership and material means that they can supply to a cause attracting large numbers of Americans, from among the main casualties of the inflationary momentum.

Material inflation itself is, of course, a way of redistributing the social product. Those who enjoy an ascendant role in the economy; whose employment of capital or skill provides a competitive advantage, ensure that the growth in their investments or income should outstrip the rise in prices and the fall in the purchasing power of money. But in order that they should have a greater share in the substance of wealth, others must have a greater share in the shadow. And for these last, therefore, the real value of their investments or income, must shrink.

Among them are those, such as so many of the disabled, the retired, the old, the widows without the will or capacity to earn, who live on fixed private incomes: through annuities from pension funds or life insurance schemes; through investments in

---

*A phrase which one of their latterday heroes, Vice-President Spiro T. Agnew, who is himself not unrepresentative of their background and outlook, has made celebrated.

government or business bonds. Having been led, by the folklore of capitalism and the propaganda of its institutions, including the state, to save safely, safety is just what they find escaping them. As the real value of their accumulated capital declines, and their income buys relentlessly less and less, they face the alternative of a terrible need or, for them, terrible resort to public help: the very dilemma which the outlook and conduct of their lives set out to avoid.

They are joined by others of their kind who were too knowledgeable for entrapment in fixed income investment, but not knowledgeable, or lucky, enough to take the right risks. Not all business corporations, even when reassuringly large, have prospered equally. Indeed, some have languished that others might the more mightily thrive. And those investors who have chosen wrongly, have watched their capital and income together slide. For them, the equity cult has proved no less a confidence trick of the system than has traditional thrift for the victims of fixed interest.

In a society which so effectively measures personal value by private consumption, such people feel themselves not only economically deprived, but personally depreciated by their material circumstances. They have worked and saved so long to maintain themselves in bereavement or retirement decently from their own resources; and the system has apparently functioned to demean them to the level of those whom they regard as the feckless poor. It is not surprising if many of them readily respond to the cry that it is the liberal corruption of capitalism which subsidizes, through inflationary social welfare, fecklessness itself, from the harvest of hard work and thrift.

Then there are the many without savings of any significance, who are totally dependent on social welfare. But social welfare is predictably slow to take adequate account of inflation, for the authorities can scarcely take such account without accordingly admitting the extent. And besides, the attempts to control the rate of inflation are in general aimed first at the public sector, and at citizens without the means to employ formidable counter-pressures. The poor may know themselves to be dependent on the welfare services of the system, but this does not mean that they are correspondingly loyal to the system itself. If they are dismayed by the ravages of material inflation, and humiliated by a prevalent morality that disparages public sources of income, then they will not easily dismiss the appeal of a new old social order, which promises to protect the deserving among them from contempt and need together, while providing their children and grandchildren with the due rewards of initiative and diligence. Thus, paradoxically, the prototypal thesis of capitalism emerges, for its adhering poor, as not less, but more protective than the welfare state of capitalism's liberal corruption; as it emerges, for its adhering rich, as involving not weaker, but stronger, and hence, surely, not smaller, but bigger government. The romanticism of the counter-revolution encloses the corporate state of private capitalism's climax.

Certainly it is the protectiveness offered by the new old social order of a purified capitalism that has manifest appeal for people so vulnerable to material inflation: who are, in a system of competitive corporate pressures, without a commensurate corporate representation of their own to promote their interests. Indeed, the more that they note the success, real or apparent, of corporate pressures, from those of big business and big labour to those of black insubordination, the more helpless and menaced they feel. A potential regime which convinced them of its capacity to represent them; or corporately to represent the nation, securing a balance between the just needs of one element and those of another, so that they themselves would not continue to be victimized for their very weakness: such would reap ready support from among their number.

And, above all perhaps, they yearn for a regime that would put an end to the progressive debasement of the moral currency, which has cost them so dear. The more that the system has promised, the less it has seemed to afford, till they are overtaken by bewilderment and despair. Elevated to being senior citizens, the old have at the same time been elevated beyond a sense of belonging to the rest of society. Encouraged to employ their leisure in developing their individual personality, they have been encouraged to seek a refuge together in special settlements, where they might not be embarrassed by, or embarrass, those younger than themselves, and where they develop in consequence only a collective depersonalization. Like widows or the disabled, they have been translated from people possessing particular common features, into particular common features possessing people. The poor come to be called the culturally disadvantaged, to relieve the disgrace of their poverty: but their poverty is not thereby relieved, and seems the more disgraceful in consequence. In short, the more language that the system has lavished on their personal needs, the less meaning such persons have found that this conveys.

Seriously assailed by the functioning of liberal capitalism, too, are the independent small-scale farmers and businessmen. Material inflation makes them all the more vulnerable to the competition of the big corporations, which have the accumulated reserves or access to credit; the resources for research and planning; the diversification for meeting setbacks; the influence over market trends, to deal, on the whole, far more successfully with rising costs or sporadic government measures of economic retrenchment. And, to be sure, the proportion of both American industry and American agriculture in the hands of the big corporations has continually increased. Yet the independent small-scale farmer and businessman are the pre-eminent heroes of American capitalist folklore and propaganda. It would be astonishing only if they were not antagonized by the discrepancy between what they are led to look for and what they find.

The lower-paid workers in industry and commerce are lower-paid precisely because their peculiar employment, their lack of skills in sufficient demand, and the weakness of their organization allow and so encourage capital to treat them accordingly.* And for the same reasons that they are the lower-paid, their earnings are the less likely to keep pace with the rate of material inflation. If capital concedes a rise in labour costs, it does so, of course, where it finds the pressures most difficult to resist: from among those whose valuable skills are combined with the militancy of self-assurance. And if it is unconcerned with the impact on existing wage differentials, this is because the workers who are able to make it concerned are not willing to do so. The result is that the earnings gap between the lower-paid and

---

*Over the decade 1950–60, according to the US Census, median wages for higher-paid 'craftsmen' rose sixty per cent; for 'semi-skilled factory workers', fifty-six per cent; and for 'service workers, laborers', thirty-nine per cent. '[The] more unskilled the worker is, the further and further behind he's been falling.' Ben J. Wattenberg in collaboration with Richard M. Scammon, *This USA*, Doubleday and Co., New York, 1965, p. 141. And the evidence suggests that this trend has, if anything, accelerated since.

the higher-paid workers tends to widen. Indeed, the lower-paid in the United States feel threatened on two fronts at once: from more valued skilled labour above them, squeezing concessions from capital at their expense; and from cheaper or unemployed black labour below them, ready to snatch their jobs if given half the chance.* For them, the assaults of material and of moral inflation are inseparable. The more that the system extols the dignity of labour and accommodates the bureaucrats of strong trade unions in the processes of decision, the more their own dignity seems denied, and their representations ignored. The more that the system tries to buy off black discontent with the pretences of racial equality, the more it seems to incite the black attack on their own jobs and earnings.

Finally among those social categories from which the commitment to counter-revolution may be expected to draw especial support, is that of public employment.† Whatever its past success in maintaining an overall material lead over workers in private industry and commerce, its ability to continue doing so must seem less and less certain, as the pressure on total resources develops. The lineaments of the crisis are all too clear in the cities, where the demands of public employees to outstrip, or at least keep pace with the rate of material inflation, can be met only by an intolerable decay of the public services or resort to a federal government whose own resources are less and less adequate to the mounting demands upon them. Attempts at restraining wage rises, by national guidelines or some other form of incomes policy, are likely to hit far harder at the public sector than at the most productive workers in the most productive industries, where strike action has so rapidly far-reaching an

---

*Obviously, the distinctions being drawn here are not absolute. There are black Americans who are old; black Americans who are independent small-scale farmers and businessmen; black Americans among the lower-paid industrial workers. It is the attitudes subjectively predominant in each such category that are objectively pertinent to an analysis of the social conflict developing in the development of the system. The mass of lower-paid industrial workers in the United States see themselves as distinct from the country's black community; as the mass of American blacks see themselves as distinct from the community of white Americans.

†This is not to say, of course, that public employees are absent from the adherents of the revolutionary commitment. The younger teachers and social workers, for instance, many of whom were first stirred into disaffection on the campus, are peculiarly well placed to appreciate the destructive impact of the system on the personality. But they are far outnumbered by those of an authoritarian outlook.

economic impact. Public employees in general can scarcely fail to see the momentum of material inflation as one which must threaten their relative living standards and corresponding social status. Furthermore, by the nature of their employment, they are supremely concerned with security and with order, in a system whose moral inflation seems supremely to be menacing both.

The police are in the front line of the fall in moral purchasing power. The more that the system claims to esteem the individual, to tolerate and even encourage dissent, and to eschew violence, the more manifest becomes its essential dependence on despising the individual, repressing dissent and utilizing violence. And if those who preside over claims and conduct alike cannot resolve the contradiction, they can at least attempt to conceal it, by condemning the conduct as they recite the claims. Like Bolingbroke in Shakespeare's *Richard II*, they 'love not poison that do poison need'. And like Exton, the police find themselves with their services duly performed, receiving 'neither . . . good word nor princely favour'.*

In this they are joined by the group in public employment that more than any other social element is historically central to authoritarian reaction: the professional military. The military order itself is informed by values scarcely compatible with those central to the civilian one of liberal capitalism. The power of property should be irrelevant, when not noxious; and the concept of representative government is the paramount heresy, as obedience is the cardinal virtue. Indeed, if the military order has, in general, so readily accepted its separation from, and status of subservience to the civilian, this is only in part because of law and custom. It is also because the military order has seen

* Exton:	Great king, within this coffin I present
	Thy buried fear: herein all breathless lies
	The mightiest of thy greatest enemies,
	Richard of Bordeaux, by me hither brought.
Bolingbroke:	Exton, I thank thee not; for thou hast wrought,
	A deed of slander with thy fatal hand
	Upon my head and all this famous land.
Exton:	From your own mouth, my lord, did I this deed.
Bolingbroke:	They love not poison that do poison need,
	Nor do I thee: though I did wish him dead,
	I hate the murderer, love him murdered.
	The guilt of conscience take thou for thy labour,
	But neither my good word nor princely favour.

Richard II, Act V.

43

its separation as helping to keep it uncontaminated by civilian values; and because it has found its status of subservience on its own terms so serviceable.

Certainly its estate has thrived: with the important role of military expenditure in civilian economic management; the essential need of the system to secure its ascendancy over much of mankind, by force where manipulation is unable to suffice; and, never pausing, preparations for the possibility of total war. Only once, when General MacArthur sought to extend the Korean fighting to the Chinese mainland, and appealed, against President Truman's decision and in defiance of his express instructions, direct to American Congressional and public opinion, did the traditional relationship of the civilian and military orders seem seriously challenged. But the Joint Chiefs of Staff opposed MacArthur's proposal, and President Truman dismissed him from command to a political storm that quickly blew itself out. The supremacy of the civilian order has not been so challenged again. And instances where individual serving military officers have intruded, beyond accepted practice, into civilian politics, have been rare and insignificant. There has been no sufficient cause for them to do so. The course of liberal capitalism has appeared to promote the interests of the military order only too well. And the military pressures of accepted practice – from Congressional lobbying in company with corporate business, to public pronouncements of circumspect occasion and wording – have usually ensured the desired adjustments.

Now, however, with the material and moral haemorrhaging of the Vietnam War and the related rise of conflict in civilian society, the professional military, like the police, are finding themselves at the centre of the developing crisis in the system. They, too, are under mounting criticism from within the liberal leadership of the civilian order; for doing, as efficiently as they believe that they can, what the system demands that they do. And they must have, in order to do what the system demands, vast numbers of young recruits, who more and more bring to military service the infectious disaffection of their civilian lives.*

*The police are beginning to experience a similar internal threat, from among their black members: a threat bound to gather force as the police are required ever more forcibly to confront the black revolutionary commitment.

Indiscipline, dissent, desertion, mutiny endanger more than the prosecution of a war; they endanger the military order itself. And this internal challenge fortifies, as it is fortified by, the external one, from within civilian society.

Increasingly the role of the military in the system is being assailed: by those who would overthrow the system altogether; by those who would rescue it by resolute reform; by those who see no other way to reduce the dangerous rate of material and moral inflation. The assault may level at the Vietnam War. But, as the professional military are themselves quick to see, there is far more than a particular war at stake. A liberal capitalism that attempted to protect itself at the cost of the military role, would become something else in the process: a system which no longer employed to mutual advantage the different concerns and values of the civilian and military orders. It would not be marvellous if there were those among the professional military who sought to head off the attempt: by promoting such changes in the system as seemed likely best to serve the security and advancement of their social role.

There remains, of course, powerful support for keeping the system as it is. The broad mass of skilled industrial and white collar labour; of those in the new technological, as of those in the old learned professions; of corporate business executives and substantial proprietors; of established bureaucrats, in the trade unions and churches, in the major political parties and the multitude of public offices: these are loyal to liberal capitalism in return for the apparent benefits that they variously enjoy. And, not least, the system that is, is: with the sustenance that this receives from cultivated inertia. Tradition, education, the institutions of continuing authority encourage people to cherish social stability rather than change, precedent rather than experiment; to settle for the devil that they know, rather than run the risk of finding themselves with a devil that they don't.

If the system could only be made to stand fast where it is, then revolution and counter-revolution alike might well be idle ideas. But the system must move. It is alive as mankind is alive; and it can as much stand still, as can the people affecting and affected

45

by it permanently hold their breath. American forces, for instance, are massively engaged in the Vietnam War. And whatever course this engagement takes, must have an impact on social challenges and stresses within the United States. Besides, the American engagement is not the only one. The Vietnamese themselves are engaged, and are no more able, even were they willing, to suspend the war somehow in mid-time. And how should they be willing? The war is no accident. It issued from a conflict of purposes; and it must continue until the conflict is resolved: by the triumph of one purpose over the other, or by some settlement that entails a measure of defeat for both.

The demand that the system makes of the world's poor is that they should rely on the remedies of liberal capitalism. They should leave to the market place and the incentives of private profit the development of their national economies, with government intervening only to prevent excesses and to encourage the process as it can. They should employ politics to accommodate, for a dynamic social stability, contending economic interests. Now, even without considering such costs of liberal capitalism as are producing a social crisis inside the very countries of its achievement, the propriety of the prescription for the poor must be doubted. For liberal capitalism is essentially a system of the rich. To the degree that it has proved so far successful, this is because the countries where it operates have had the means to eliminate mass destitution among their own citizens, and provide a sufficiently widespread further rise in living standards. And this they have done in large part through the capital equipment, in skills and machinery, of advanced industrialization. But the acquisition of such equipment, the very existence of advanced industrialization may in turn significantly be traced to the vast surplus for investment produced by past exploitation of the poor world: whether directly, through conquest; or indirectly, through economic dominance. What, for instance, early industrialization in Britain owed to the triangular trade* is well enough known.

*Manufacturers exchanged at a profit for slaves in Africa; slaves exchanged at a profit for raw materials in the Americas; raw materials shipped back to be processed at a profit in Britain, for sale or exchange across the world.

And similar exploitation, however refined its present character, persists. For such, too, is a prerequisite of the prosperity which allows liberal capitalism to function at home as it does. The United States, for instance, may exchange manufactures, at a profit, for rubber in Liberia; process the rubber, at a profit, in American company plants; and then exchange the product, at a profit, for tin from Bolivia or coffee from Brazil. But, of course, the economic patterns are often far more complex; with several rich countries on one side, and several poor ones on the other, engaged in a series of transactions that basically involve the exchange of manufactures for raw materials (or, of more elaborate and costly manufactures for more primitive and cheaper ones) to the consistent profit of the rich.

The prescription offered by liberal capitalism to the poor ignores or conceals, therefore, some rather pertinent factors. The poor have no vast accumulated surplus invested in the equipment, human and material, of advanced industrialization. They have no trading advantages with which profitably to exploit the rich. They have no weak foreign peoples from whom to derive resources, directly through colonial conquest or indirectly through economic dominance. They have only themselves from whom to squeeze a large enough surplus for the cost of acquiring the necessary machines and skills.

Yet, even this formidable endeavour is made more formidable still, by the requirement of the already rich countries to be rewarded for their participation. The poor have to provide not only a surplus for domestic investment, but a priority surplus for adequate payment to the foreign companies operating among them. And this payment is certainly no less a loss to the countries from which it is taken, than it is of gain to the countries which receive it, through the earnings of company personnel, through

'The triangular trade . . . gave a triple stimulus to British industry. The negroes were purchased with British manufactures; transported to the plantations, they produced sugar, cotton, indigo, molasses and other tropical products, the processing of which created new industries in England; while the maintenance of the negroes and their owners on the plantations provided another market for British industry, New England agriculture and the Newfoundland fisheries. By 1750 there was hardly a trading or a manufacturing town in England which was not in some way connected with the triangular or direct colonial trade. The profits obtained provided one of the main streams of that accumulation of capital in England which financed the Industrial Revolution.' Eric Williams, *Capitalism and Slavery*, University of North Carolina Press, 1944, p. 52.

the dividends to stockholders, and through the nourishment of other, connected industry.

To be sure, there is no credible prospect of rescue through the realities of aid from liberal capitalist resources. At the start of the 'sixties, the United Nations, with the prerequisite agreement of the rich, launched a development decade. But in 1969, the Commission on International Development, headed by Lester Pearson, a former prime minister of Canada, reported that aid given by these countries had dwindled from 0.89 per cent of their combined gross national products at the outset of the decade, to 0.77 per cent in 1968; alongside the almost meaninglessly low objective of an annual 1.0 per cent.[1] Moreover, the composition of such aid had also deteriorated. Aid provided in grant or 'grant-like' form declined from $4.5 billion in 1961 to $4.1 billion in 1968 – the decline in real value was, with inflation, much sharper – when the poor were already returning to the rich over $4 billion a year in the mere servicing of debts. By 1968, almost half the aid consisted of investment and commercial credit: which, as the Pearson Commission rightly pointed out, should not be termed 'aid' at all. And, of the remaining half, the proportion made up by loans had tripled. All but a sixth of the total aid was tied to purchases in a particular country among the rich: a practice which, the commission estimated, usually reduced the value of such aid by more than twenty per cent. And a fifth of the total aid consisted of surplus food and commodities, which scarcely involved the rich in any sacrifice, and did not notably augment the productive capacities of the poor. During the same period, the rich countries had doubled their combined gross national products, to a total of $1,700 billion.

If Marx was wrong in predicting the polarization of capital and labour, with a revolutionary destitute proletariat inside industrial society, how wrong was he for the society of mankind? From 1958 to 1965, for instance, the rich 'market' economies of the world, with a low birth rate, increased their share, of combined gross domestic products, from 82.8 per cent to 83.9 per cent: while the share of the poor or 'developing' ones, with a higher birth rate, fell from 17.2 per cent to 16.1 per cent.* True, this higher birth rate may itself promote the poverty of

*Figures from U.N. Statistical Office yearbooks.

the poor. But, as such statistics make plain, the poverty is promoted anyway. For the rich, indeed, the emphasis on birth control by the poor is too commonly an occasion for evading or denying other, less congenial truths.

So many countries of the poor world are economically stagnant or decaying, because such progress as they have been capable of making is squandered in high, sterile consumption by the various indigenous elites. These last need no lessons in the private material impulse from the rich of liberal capitalism. Mexico and Peru, supposed instances of some capitalist success, now each has a gross national product of over $300 a head; and had an average annual economic growth rate of more than six per cent between 1960 and 1967. But each also reveals dangerously wide social inequalities: with a relatively very few rich of landowning, industry, trade and government; and a mass either sunken in servitude to the earth or swelling the squalor of the city slums.*

Such countries are not independent experiments in liberal capitalism. They are essentially its colonies. And they are colonies whose social product is thus doubly taxed: to provide what may be termed the metropolitan economy of the system, with substantial returns from trade, investments in industry and commerce, private and public loans; and substantially both to reward and to protect the colonial clientele of imperial control. Indeed, government to administer the colonial processes through a multitude of bureaucrats, and with the ministers of coercion in the police and the army, has become, for most countries of the poor, the fastest developing if least productive sector of the economy.

In the context of this profound material exploitation, the much-promised 'economic miracle', or break-through to self-generating industrial growth, is a propaganda deceit. Certainly the model of Japan is a mirage. It is not merely that the Japanese undertook their great leap forward more than a century ago, when the costs were comparatively so much lower, and the international competition was so much less fierce, than now. But at the time, under the Meiji imperial regime, Japan itself

*See, for instance, a report on Mexico in the *Financial Times*, London, 10 November 1969, which mentions 'the long-term threat posed by the contrast between rich and poor (which is *not* being reduced although this has been an ostensible aim of recent Governments)...'

was not paying tribute to suzerain foreign capital and to the local agents of this suzerainty. In its social isolation, it was morally feudal. Its elite emphasized the obligations as well as the prerogatives of power: and far from being engaged in a spree of competitive display, was puritanical in its resolve to construct a strong industrial economy and defeat the threat of Western armed intervention.* Where are its parallels in the poor world today: with the elites only recognizing the morality of private consumption, and no obligations beyond service to their own prerogatives? And even where, rarely, the colonial regimes do set out to reduce their dependence by radical initiatives, the system is quick to bribe or coerce them back into line.

The representative predicament of the poor is that of India. There, one peaceful revolution after the other, within the imperial orbit, has been acclaimed by the prophets of liberal capitalism; and proved all too soon the occasion mainly for augmenting the resources of the elite. The latest hope, in the 'green revolution' of more productive food strains, well illustrates the problem. For it is not dissipating but sharpening the Indian social crisis: as the prospect of more profitable agriculture encourages private efficiency and increased unemployment in the countryside without any corresponding increase in urban jobs. It is the already rich who have the means and see the advantages of exploiting the new possibilities: and while they grow richer in consequence, to engage in yet more lavish consumption, the poverty and despair of the populace deepen. It is scarcely surprising that at last there are signs, as with the Naxilites, of revolutionary endeavour, encouraged by the example of a Maoist China.

Of course, poverty itself is not necessarily rebellious. The world has long displayed, and India pre-eminently within it, a poverty listless and submissive. It is the awareness of deprivation, rather, that arouses resentment and resistance. And today the mobility of knowledge through mass communications and, not least, the salesmanship of the market place, is opening up the world as never before. Liberal capitalism becomes its own worst enemy. The poor are made more and more aware – through radio, television, films, vernacular books and newspapers, ad-

---

*And soon enough, too, of course, it took the Western road to empire, with its main thrust into China.

vertising, report and rumour – of the relatively high living standards enjoyed by the populace of the rich world, and by their own rich. And they grow accordingly less acquiescent in their lot and in the looting to which their elites are directed.

Inevitably involved in the material, is the moral exploitation of the system's imperial theme. The colonial regime starts by reflecting the same pretensions to personal freedom, equal opportunity, social justice, as does the metropolitan: but there is manifestly still less force to the imported forms. As the promise of the polls appears more and more elusive; the ceremony of democratic procedure, more and more a mask: so the sense of moral outrage is fired. And as disaffection develops, the promise and the ceremony are sooner or later packed away; and the ballot box gives place to the gun. Yet this can only accelerate the erosion of popular acquiescence in the dominance of the system. From behind the local clients it approves or tolerates, it stands revealed as violence, irreclaimable; and the response that it predictably produces is a revolutionary commitment to overcome it.

This commitment is ultimately an assertion of independent personality: a searching to shatter the subservience that informs the various social, and through them individual, relationships with metropolitan power. That is why it is not always the poor, but indeed often those on the edges of the elite or even inside, who lead the insurgency. Capitalism itself, with its idealism of property, comes to represent the total captivity of colonial man. It stands for the metropolitan domination of his economy: through established terms of trade, which perpetuate the bondage of raw material suppliers to metropolitan markets; through the pressures of amassed debt and continuing credit; through the intimidation, defeat or absorption of local enterprise by metropolitan corporations. It stands for the metropolitan domination of politics: whether from without, through economic, diplomatic, military controls; or from within, through the institutions and conventions of power that convey the peculiar values of the system. It stands for the metropolitan domination of culture: from the priorities of private consumption, to the objectives and methods of education; the ideas and very language of government and constitutional opposition. In short, it stands for a new colonialism, with the system now, more pervasively, if covertly, in the place of the old overt national imperialisms: but a new colonialism that has only developed out of the old, to combine the humiliations and denials of the past with those of the present for a cumulative affront to the future.

As the captivity excites resistance, so the resistance must excite attempts to crush it: for the material and moral challenge that it constitutes not only in itself, but in the impact of its example. To be sure, the United States, as the principal if not the sole protector of the system's ascendancy, does not rush to confront every manifestation of such resistance with its own armed forces. There are many instruments available. Collapsing client governments may, for a time, be shored up by money and by military equipment and advice; while professing revolutionary regimes may be held or returned to allegiance by economic disruption or the fomenting and fuelling of internal assaults. But in the end the system must be ready to engage in other Vietnams and suffer the consequences; or suffer the consequences of refusing to do so. Its dilemma is intrinsic and hence inescapable. It cannot withdraw from its foreign domain without changing in the process; and it cannot attempt to maintain itself there without a cost that must change it in the very attempt. The challenge it faces abroad fortifies and is fortified by the challenge it faces at home. Its domestic material and moral inflation must mount, to promote the revolutionary commitment and the self-destructive rescue of counter-revolution.

With the open American military intervention in Cambodia, the building workers who gathered in Wall Street, to demonstrate support for their government and its policies, were not only reacting to the protests that raged on the campuses. They chose Wall Street deliberately, because the plunge in stock prices seemed to betray a demoralization within the ranks of the bourgeoisie itself. It was an event the rich symbolism of which at once denied the particular Marxist prognosis of social conflict under capitalism, and asserted the critical reach of such conflict none the less. For here were todays unmistakeable workers calling upon capital to have confidence in, and help them to sustain, its own system. They were right to be anxious.

No social system can long survive the loss of corporate self-assurance among the broad mass of its leadership. And what doubt can there be that the broad mass of the bourgeoisie are losing the will, along with the belief in their ability, to save liberal capitalism from itself? One factor is that the revolt against their values increasingly recruits, as it has unprecedentedly been raised by, their own children. Capitalism itself contains a crucial hereditary element. Indeed, if the triumph of the system was marked by a decline in the acknowledged power and glory of God, this was partly because property appeared to offer a rather more convincing prospect of immortality than did prayer.* The disaffection of its own young is thus doubly disturbing to the bourgeoisie: it denies not only the moral principles, but a vital psychical impulse of capitalism. A man, it is said, builds for his son. But what if his son despises the building?

And what, moreover, if he and his fellows seem set on actually demolishing it? For the challenge is physical as well as psychical, and it is sufficiently immediate. The young demonstrators can scarcely be ignored when they begin to interfere with the functioning of the system: by fracturing the conduct of higher education; using the streets for turbulent complaint; impeding the processes of national defence; invading the citadels of business with sit-ins, and with clamour at stockholder meetings; even burning and bombing property. To ignore must be to encourage their defiance. Yet how are they to be checked? To send police or the National Guard, for the protection of law and order, against black rebels in the ghetto, is one thing; to send police or the National Guard against white rebels on the campus and in the streets, is another. What social leadership comfortably countenances the risk of bludgeoning and shooting its own children? And after the Kent State University killings, who in the social leadership can dismiss the terrible reality of the risk?

But the draining morale of the bourgeoisie has much to do, too, with the changing nature of their relationship to the means production. As more and more of the economy has fallen under the sway of the major corporations, the role of proprietor-

*The immortality may be qualified by the impositions of estate tax. But these have remained manageable enough to maintain the principle.

management has correspondingly diminished. The prosperous bourgeois today, even if still with a factory, shop or professional practice of his own, is likely to have much of his capital invested in an assortment of stocks, from a prudent variety of big corporations. He may well suppose himself richer, and more securely rich, than he would otherwise have been. But he knows that he is, to that degree, in the hands of others. The condition of his power is, paradoxically, his powerlessness. He has become more a consumer than a producer; more an employee than an employer; more an instrument than an agent of wealth. And what is true of the economy is relatedly true of the polity. As the activities of government have expanded, to regulate the economy and preserve or procure requisite social support for the system, the broad mass of the bourgeoisie have seen the processes of decision recede from their grasp. If the black and the young were not consulted over American military involvement in Vietnam, neither were they. And if the periodic contest between the Republican and Democratic parties for the right to preside, seems ultimately meaningless to so many of the young and the black, many of the bourgeois would be hard put to say why it should hold much meaning for them.

Surely, if they are so bewildered, so uncertain now of their hold on history, it is because they are more than a little convinced by the arguments of disaffection. Their own experience confirms the claim that social control is increasingly exercised by a managerial elite unaccountable and unresponsive to the accepted democratic decencies. Did not Eisenhower himself give solemn warning of the military-industrial complex? Was not Kennedy persuaded into the unprofitable, potentially disastrous adventure of the Cuban Bay of Pigs, on the erroneous advice of an electorally irresponsible intelligence establishment? Did not Johnson plunge the United States yet deeper in the Vietnamese morass by a series of deceptions, in which he was partly the deceiver and partly himself the deceived? And by what public consultations did Nixon decide that the morass should be extended to Cambodia?

It was not they, the proper leaders of a propertied democracy, who wanted or determined that their society should become so racked with violence; that the corruptions of crime should so spread as to make even the school a market place for hard drugs; that prosperity should involve the stubborn pollution of their lives, by greed and loneliness and distrust, as it stubbornly pollutes the very air they breathe with the waste products of profit. How did it happen that they should so feel themselves now the helpless objects of a social mechanism with a movement, a will of its own? that the same property which was to enhance their sense of individual value and liberty, should have deprived them of it instead? None of this is what the system promised. And are they faithfully to protect a system that has proved so faithless?

But if they should desert it, where would they go? The revolutionary commitment plays on their bewilderment, their uncertainty; and because it comes so often from their own children, its peculiar disaffection may be adopted by some of them also, if only no further than a desperate connivance. But playing on their bewilderment, their uncertainty, too, is the counter-revolutionary commitment. And this appeals in terms of a social ordering, a structure of civilization, based on the prerogatives of property and the developed principles of the past, that the bourgeois have been brought up to appreciate. It offers no prospect of perilous, even perpetual social experiment; no trusting to an imagination that they have been taught conscientiously to distrust: but instead a social investment in restraint, a vigorous authoritarianism that will restore a sense of personal direction and control over the social mechanism. It will reestablish general confidence in the moral and material currency of capitalism; and so deny revolution, abroad and at home, its primary impulse. No longer will the bourgeois need to risk having their own children beaten or shot on the campus or in the streets, and sent year after year to be maimed or killed in foreign battle. Order will be enforced until its acceptance will be natural. Its very repressions will liberate. It will give back faith.

As the social consensus breaks up, it is all too probable that the bulk of the bourgeoisie will be drawn to support, or at least to acquiesce in, the counter-revolutionary assault on liberalism. There is abundant evidence already of this drift. Yet to propose that the likely principal agent and heir of the system's collapse will be counter-revolution is not to know the particular shape that this will take. To conjure up a model from the past,

55

as of Nazi Germany for instance, is to invite justifiable derision. And contemporary precedents, in the colonial orbit of the system, from Nigeria to Brazil, are scarcely blueprints for the United States. Overt military rule is not the only form an authoritarian regime can take. Nor, indeed, is authoritarianism, however extreme, incompatible with the regularly expressed sentiment of a numerical majority. The Soviet Union of Stalin was no less Stalinist for the allegiance of the multitude. It is far from inconceivable that in countries of liberal capitalism, an increasingly despotic regime should emerge in the custody of an established constitutional party: the new order in the old clothes of the polls.

This scenario of crisis in the system has so far concentrated on the United States. And there are obvious reasons for this. The country so dominates the economic life of liberal capitalism everywhere, that any other in the system must be correspondingly affected by profound changes in American society. And this economic predominance is matched by a military one. There is much justice in the mounting American complaint that other countries in the system enjoy the benefits of military exertions by the United States without shouldering a proportionate share of the costs. It is true that Britain and France, for instance, each to its supposed advantage, defend particular areas of invest-ment and influence abroad. But these engagements are peripheral. It is the United States, by the fear or force of its military dispositions, that ultimately secures the empire of liberal capitalism for French and British, German and Japanese, Swiss and Swedish – along with American – private enterprise. And, above all, the predominance of the United States is moral. One need only ask what the probable impact would be on the ideological climate in other countries of the system, were the United States to fall under fascism, or find its way at last to the proper politics of personality.

This does not mean that the social experience of the United States must be mirrored everywhere else in the system. For each country has a distinctive past, a distinctive political and economic character such as to influence the course of the crisis in liberal capitalism there. Switzerland has pursued the principles of national neutrality and banking secrecy, to become a refuge for foreign funds; as Norway has not. Neither Switzerland nor Norway possesses a recent imperial grandeur, to the vanishing of whose glow so many citizens of Britain or France have had such difficulty in adapting themselves. The established Roman Catholic Church in Italy plays a direct political role to which the established Church of England has long ceased even to aspire. Canada and Belgium have internal conflicts along linguistic regional lines, by contrast with which most countries in the system seem each remarkably homogeneous. The communist party commands the bulk of trade union membership and of labour votes in Italy and France, though elsewhere under liberal capitalism it achieves at best a significant minority of both. In Italy, a largely agricultural, economically depressed south has been drained by a flow of workers not only to the booming industries of the north, but as temporary migrants to those of neighbouring countries. The West German and Swiss economies have flourished on just such infusions of migrant foreign labour, mainly from the poorer parts of Europe. Both France and Britain now have, drawn from various former colonies, considerable immigrant communities, around whose peculiar colour, customs, and concentration in certain areas of employment and residence, racial stresses are gathering. Yet these stresses are at present far more manifest and menacing in Britain than in France.

What differentiates these countries from one another, and each from the United States, is not to be dismissed. Yet many existing differences are due to no more than respective leads and lags in the development of liberal capitalism itself. The American urban momentum, with far-flung suburbs merging at their edges to make the immuring megalopolis, has become a seemingly irresistible model for one country in the system after another. If industrial pollution once appeared an eccentrically American exercise in destructive pioneering, West Germany, or Belgium, or the Netherlands is not now far behind, and Japan is racing ahead. If public services, from schools and transport to garbage collection, seem less and less adequate to the mounting demands upon their neglect in the United States, where else in the system is this process not in some measure evident? The American ratio of crime and especially of violence may comfort other countries under liberal capitalism with their relative backwardness in both; but their own growth rates suggest that they are following fast in American tracks. If the social mechanism seems to have got so dismayingly beyond the comprehension of the individual citizen in the United States, it is scarcely more comprehensible elsewhere in the system. And, ultimately, though the assault of moral and material inflation may differ in degree from one such country to another, it exists, with its inevitable consequences for social conflict, in all.

But the system promotes a fundamental identity of social experience among its separate states not only through its intrinsic purposes and operations. Because it is fundamentally a single system to which these states belong, social communication between one and another is accordingly close. If new industrial techniques and developments in business management spread so easily across national frontiers, how should new techniques of social manipulation, or developments in disaffection indeed, be contained within them? There must be few, if any, countries under liberal capitalism where constitutional politics have not been influenced by the packaged magic of John F. Kennedy's career: so that the very word 'Kennedy' has come to stand for the merchandizing of a youthful and adventurous electoral image.

Certainly there are few, if any, such countries where resistance to the social order has not been excited or affected by the ideas and methods of revolt in the United States. And, of course, the traffic is not one-way. The British Campaign for Nuclear Disarmament; the surge of West German student demonstrations in 1967; the tumultuous events of May – June 1968 in France; the movement of protest, across the system, against the American military involvement in Vietnam: each had its impact, however apparently delayed, on the growth of social mutiny in the United States. For whenever the system is seen to be challenged from within, challenge itself is encouraged; and the course of one engagement becomes appropriate preparation for another.

These challenges need not begin as such. They become so, as the specific social grievances from which they arise are seen to have their source in the very nature of the system. The Catholics of Northern Ireland have been drawn to revolt by a Protestant dominance which has long discriminated against them in the allotment of housing and jobs, as in the composition of local government. Yet in the course of a revolt explicitly for equal civil rights, the responsibility of liberal capitalism, for sustaining a religious division through the competitive dynamic, has increasingly been identified. The resolve of Protestants to retain, as the resolve of Catholics to resist, the Protestant ascendancy, owes much to the relatively depressed economic condition of Northern Ireland, where jobs and decent housing are scarcer than in most regions of the United Kingdom, and where the struggle to obtain or keep them is commensurately fierce. There is, thus, a significant parallel with racial conflict in the United States. For just as opposition there to the prospect of social advance by blacks is strongest among lower-income whites, who see their jobs and superior racial status endangered, so in Northern Ireland it is the Protestants with meanly paid and insecure jobs or no jobs at all who most strongly oppose demands by Catholics for social advance. And, in the event, the leadership of the Catholic revolt, as of the black in the United States, has turned more and more of its fire from the manifestations of the system to the system itself.

There is a further parallel of significance. The black and student revolts in the United States emerged to social moment under the formally progressive administrations of John F. Kennedy and Lyndon B. Johnson: administrations which revealed, by the flare of their own rhetoric, how barrenly repressive the reformism of social democracy had become in its attachment to the priorities of property. And similarly it was no accident that Catholic resistance in Northern Ireland, like nationalist movements in Scotland and Wales, should have reached such prominence under the Labour government of Harold Wilson in the United Kingdom. As acceptable capitalist techniques of economic retrenchment, to secure first the old and then the new exchange rate of sterling, were deployed; and the dictates of the market place, appropriately transmitted; unemployment figures rose to levels unrecorded since the first year of the Second World War. And, of course, given the functioning of the system, by which those in front prosper at the expense of those behind, it was the areas of industrial backwardness like Northern Ireland, Scotland and Wales, that suffered most. It was not astonishing that they should have nurtured a search for some radical escape from the dead-end of conventional politics under liberal capitalism.

That nationalism itself provides no such escape, the career of the nation state within the system should by now have sufficiently demonstrated. And the nationalist parties of Scotland and Wales – as the nationalist constituency in the Northern Ireland Catholic revolt – have betrayed the trap of the nationalist impulse in the underlying ideological confusions of their cause. Yet however this impulse has been and will be expressed there, or elsewhere under liberal capitalism,* it represents a profound discontent with the manifestations of the system: from the depersonalizing inequalities of competitive riches and poverty, to the depersonalizing processes of bureaucratic central government. Indeed, this nationalism is a yearning for personality, if only for the illusion of individual personality through the personality of a new nation state. And sooner or later, this impulse must be seen, by more and more of those who experience it, for the trap that it is; with hostility to particular manifestations of the system becoming a commitment to displace the system itself, by the investment in a citizenship of man. For some, as in Northern Ireland, who have found themselves so irrelevantly caught, the moral readjustment has already begun.

But meanwhile such movements of rebellious nationalist yearning constitute yet one more threat to the stability of the system and promote the counter-revolutionary commitment in reaction. And there are other challenges promoting the commitment which are still helplessly, passively such. If an invigorated racism among the lower-income and socially less secure whites in the United States in the answer to militant demands for effective racial equality by indigenous blacks, a similar development among the lower-income and socially less secure whites in Britain is due rather to the mere presence of a large immigrant coloured community. Resentment and anxiety, at rising unemployment and poor housing, at overcrowded classrooms in the schools and overcrowded wards in the hospitals, at all the failures which successive governments have so glibly excused, seize on the coloured immigrant as somehow

*As among those of the regional French culture in Canada, for instance; or among the Flemish in Belgium.

responsible. And, as in the United States, the issue of disorder joins that of race, for an assault, by the moralists of a purified capitalism, on some vast conspiracy to exploit social decadence and subvert the state.

Enoch Powell, a one-time professor and now a prominent Conservative politician, acquired a considerable personal following, especially among white manual workers, for his pronouncements on the dangers of coloured immigration. By the general election campaign of 1970, he was warning of concerted secret moves against law and order, the culture, the nation: of an enemy which excited turbulence in the universities; which had infiltrated the civil service to disguise the real growth rate of the coloured community; which exploited a perplexed liberalism and a gratuitously guilt-ridden Christianity.

Elsewhere in the system, when no substantial coloured community is present to fuel the counter-revolutionary appeal, migrant foreign workers may provide a suitable substitute. And, to be sure, the prodigious increase in their numbers, at the insistent call of industry, has made the stirring up of indigenous disquiet all too easy. In 1959 there were barely ten thousand such workers in West Germany; in 1970 there were some 1,670,000, including 350,000 Italians, 326,000 Yugoslavs, and 290,000 Turks.[2] And if the social stresses that resulted seemed unimportant in the boom years following, they had been somewhat less so in 1966, when the economy faltered.

But then the fear of mounting unemployment may sometimes serve for the fact; and the system generates other encouragements enough, in the career of material and moral inflation, to find, with the appropriate guidance, a scapegoat in the foreign labour force. Fed by foreign workers, to the point where they had come to constitute some 16 per cent of the total population, the Swiss economy flourished. But this did not stop James Schwarzenbach, a Zurich deputy with a high formal education that furthered the resemblance to Enoch Powell in Britain, from achieving considerable support for a campaign severely to reduce their numbers. With the signatures of sufficient voters, his proposals were submitted to a national referendum. And the contest that followed was, albeit in the absence of a significant revolutionary commitment, otherwise remarkably representative of the social conflict developing in countries under liberal capitalism.

The leadership of corporate business made strenuous efforts to defeat the Schwarzenbach initiative. It employed to the utmost its influence in the press and other mass communications; it paid for lavish advertisements, on the dire consequences for the Swiss economy that would attend acceptance of the proposals; and individual large companies reinforced the warnings by timely announcements of plans to shift investment and production abroad. The rest of the liberal establishment, including the churches, the major trade unions and political parties, the government itself, variously confronted the challenge. Indeed, in March 1970, three months before the proposals were due for decision, the government made a pre-emptive bid. It limited the inflow of foreign workers to 40,000 a year. And since some 80,000 such workers had been returning home annually, this promised to reduce the total numbers by some 160,000 in four years; or to achieve over half the four-year reduction of 300,000 demanded by Schwarzenbach.

Yet, in the event, the proposals were still supported by an overall forty-six per cent of the voters, in a seventy-four per cent poll, and carried seven of the twenty-two cantons. Heavily industrialized cantons, like Zurich itself, recorded a majority, if hardly a crushing one, against the Schwarzenbach initiative. And in five of the seven cantons where the initiative was approved, the foreign labour force already made up less than ten per cent of the population, or the local limit that Schwarzenbach had sought to impose. If, therefore, the number of foreign workers was a source of discontent in itself, it was clearly also an issue for the expression of other discontents. A correspondent of the London *Economist* identified electoral categories of resentment at the way in which the system was functioning.

'It seems to have been the farmers, the lower-paid industrial workers, the minor civil servants and the struggling independent craftsmen who used the occasion to express their hostility towards a government which appears to them to pay more attention to industry and banking than to less privileged parts of the community.'[8]

Inevitably, the same conciliating measures introduced to defeat the Schwarzenbach proposals will markedly sharpen the challenges to itself that the system provokes. Each canton now has a specific annual quota of foreign workers, in place of the individual company quotas that previously applied; while the foreign workers themselves are now permitted to change their jobs after one year, or after three years their canton and type of employment. The larger and stronger companies are likely to take advantage of the increased labour mobility and pressures for mechanization, at the expense of the smaller and weaker ones; as the richer cantons are likely to thrive at the expense of the poorer. Simultaneously, labour may be expected to take advantage of its enhanced scarcity, in wresting higher earnings: with an internal vying that must favour those of more valued skills and effective organization at the expense of their fellows. And connectedly, throughout, inflation will further erode the relative living standards and status of important groups in Swiss society: to promote the revolt from a radical right against the system.

Nor is it reasonably to be supposed that the challenge of coloured or foreign labour communities will forever remain as helpless, as passive, as it has so far commonly been. Coloured immigrants in Britain are predictably being aroused by the racial discriminations, within or in defiance of the law, that they suffer. More and more, theirs is the black American experience: with statutory assurances of their equal rights only emphasizing the actual social denials; with their prevalently low incomes and the flight of whites at their approach, placing or keeping them in central city ghettoes; with their children in neighbourhood and hence increasingly coloured schools; with the self-perpetuations of poverty made the more outrageous by the humiliations of race. To be sure, they constitute not one community of colour, but several: separated from each other along cultural, religious, even residually linguistic lines, according to the countries in Asia, the Caribbean and Africa, from which the immigrants have come. But they are being drawn defensively together: under the impact of the dominant host culture, with its racist strain; and of ideas, such as 'black power', reaching them through their intelligentsia and the mass media of the society at large. And in this, the immigrant experience is, too, much like that of colour in the United States, where the walls separating from each other 'Negro' and 'Red Indian' and 'Mexican' and 'Puerto Rican' have begun to tumble under the trumpeting of a shared disaffection.

The European foreign worker usually identifies himself with his homeland: where so often he has left a wife and children behind, and sends much of his earnings. He expects, by the terms of his stay, to go; and comes, therefore, prepared to disregard any experience of exclusion from what the indigenous see as their prerogatives. He is concerned to get on with his job; and is all too aware of his vulnerability to sudden deportation, should he ever be considered more trouble than he is worth. Yet, correspondingly, his conditions of work, of accommodation, of leisure, are generally inferior to those enjoyed by the mass of citizen labour. Time itself makes the contrast less and less acceptable; and the antagonism that he feels directed, so unprovoked, towards him, from among those whose superior living standards he serves, incites his own. In West Germany, for instance, students in the revolutionary movement have had some little success in encouraging strikes and other demonstrations of discontent among foreign workers. And though such has scarcely challenged the security of the system, even at the remove of the authoritarian response, how should it continue long to be so?

Finally, if the ideas and techniques of the revolutionary commitment spread easily from one part of the system to another, the ideas and techniques of counter-revolution are not likely to find it more difficult. The course of social conflict in the United States must itself be affected by, as it affects, the course in other countries under liberal capitalism. And if some of these seem socially more stable than the United States, for not having reached the American level of systematic development, others may be less so, paradoxically for the same reason.

In Italy, corporate business and trade union bureaucracy are not as integrated in the manipulative processes of government. And the conciliations of social welfare are yet further behind the albeit lower demand: in part because the social product itself is proportionately so much smaller; and in part because the taxation of wealth is effectively still less progressive. Given the remnants of feudalism, especially in the south; the posture of the Vatican, with one foot in the Counter-Reformation and the other in the American century; a capitalist attachment to the heyday of unregulated accumulation, and a social democratic movement already as bankrupt as its counterparts elsewhere; a communist party with its gaze fixed on the staircase of constitutional power, and the consequent heretics of a revolutionary alternative; the legacies of, and the allegiances to, the earlier resolutions of fascism: Italian politics present a sort of chronological disorder, by which different periods in the development of capitalism clash and combine to produce corresponding compromises with the requirements of the system. And the system itself is sufficiently established for its material and moral inflationary momentum to make each successive compromise further occasion for conflict: with the competitive pressures for rising private consumption all the sharper for the shortcomings in the public services; with those weaker in the struggle to wrest concessions, all the more deprived and humiliated; and with the forces of revolution and of counter-revolution fostering each other. There are few social prospects that may sensibly be ruled out: and if among those that may not be, one is a grand coalition of corporate business, the communist party and the Church, for an attempt at saving the system through serious reform; another is the capture of the state by the counter-revolutionary impulse, with varying measures of instigation, support and connivance from an anxious Church and a distraught bourgeoisie.

For so long successful in the politics of accommodation, Britain now, too, is increasingly reflecting the crisis in the system. With gathering public bewilderment and alarm at the cumulative failure of liberal capitalism to fulfil its promise, and especially at the ravages of the inflationary momentum, the new Conservative government is engaged on a programme of counter-reformism. Ready, if as yet more measuredly than the Powellites in the party, to flourish the need of a menaced social order, it is seeking to bring labour under more rigorous corporate control, directly by statute and indirectly by the disciplines of a higher unemployment rate. Profitable sectors of nationalized industry are being sold off to private enterprise. Taxation is being made less progressive to enhance material incentives; and the cause of industrial efficiency served by less public assistance for backward areas or ailing businesses. Welfare services are more and more being subjected to the principle of a 'means test', or the demonstration of sufficient poverty. Competition is to be freed from many of the restraints which the system has so liberally developed: while the state resolves corporate conflicts and secures the national interest. It is a counter-reformism that must nourish the counter-revolutionary commitment with the very resistance it meets and with the disappointment of the hopes it raises. And given the particularly close cultural relationship between the two countries, this may be expected to have a powerful impact on politics in the United States.

Certainly nowhere has the crisis in liberal capitalism, with the clash of revolutionary and counter-revolutionary commitments, reached as far as in France.

By the spring of 1958, the Fourth Republic was gangrenous with the Algerian war. A medley of parties and factions governed through a series of uneasy alliances: that eschewed any participation by the communist party from the parliamentary left; and that was assailed, from the parliamentary far right, by the Poujadist movement, with its main support among small shop-keepers, and by the more fanatic representatives of the settler ascendancy in Algeria. The 'classical' right, without whose support no coalition could thus command enough votes in the National Assembly, resisted, along with its kin in the small Gaullist party, the prospect of any imperial retreat from Algeria. And as premier succeeded premier, to represent the leadership now of the Socialists, now of one or other faction among the Radicals, the regime grew more repressive and unauthoritative at once. While the latest government appeased the right and antagonized liberal opinion, by confiscating publications and prosecuting respectable citizens for undermining the Algerian engagement, it neither prevented nor punished a noisy demonstration, by one thousand Paris police, outside and against the National Assembly itself. And more menacing than the police, many of the professional military, embittered by the defeat in Indo-China, the withdrawal from Tunisia and Morocco, and the fiasco of the 1956 Suez war, were increasingly contrasting the needs of victory in Algeria with the incompetence of metropolitan politics.

The Algerian war was not the crisis of the system in France: any more than the Vietnam war has been the crisis of the system in the United States. But, as the Vietnam war subsequently for the United States, it was an essential aspect of this crisis. What was then manifestly at issue was the role of the old imperialism in the changing capitalist dominion. To accept the loss of Algeria, the prime imperial prize that had been made constitutionally an inseparable part of metropolitan France, was to accept the loss, however piecemeal, of the whole French empire: with the surrender not only of the colonial contribution to French prosperity, but of the world status and influence in which so much French history was invested. Yet to go on with the war would be to go on draining France of men and money: until popular opinion rose to overwhelm the responsible politicians; or the republic fell to those for whom popular opinion was irrelevant, and the fate of the responsible politicians already sealed. Without the empire, how was France to escape becoming an ultimate satellite of the United States? And with the costs that securing the empire now seemed to involve, how was France to escape deepening economic dependence on the United States?

The communist party had its own version of the dilemma. A retreat by France from Algeria might mean only the displacement of French by American suzerainty there; and this, the Soviet government had no doubts, was scarcely in the interests of the world working-class movement. The French workers themselves, so long guided by the party, seemed less than ardent to run economic and political risks for the sake of their colonial comrades. And, in any event, the immediate danger, which militant opposition to the war might only succeed in making irresistible, came from the far right and the army. Yet the war itself fed the very forces which aimed at seizing the state. And how could the party accommodate the cause of imperial rule over Algeria, without in the process embarrassing too far its residual revolutionary claims? What remained was to denounce the war, while doing nothing effectively to weaken the social order that presided over its prosecution.

Militant opposition there was, from an incipient new left of intellectuals, students, young conscripts. But it was from within the ranks of the liberal bourgeoisie, and not least from the higher reaches of corporate business, that the search for a settlement with Algerian nationalism most influentially came. Here there was a welcome for the pressing American offers of mediation:

as there was a recognition that the promise of capitalism in France lay in industrial vigour; in exploiting the opportunities of the new European Economic Community; in preserving the advantages of empire by conceding the ceremonial of independence; and in leaving to the leadership and resources of the United States, the defence of capitalism against any crucial revolutionary challenge. Indeed, it was with the latest American offer of mediation, in the international storm that followed the Sakhiet incident*, that the government of Felix Gaillard moved hopefully towards some rescue from the Algerian predicament; and by so moving, was brought down in the National Assembly.

Another government with a similar policy, led from the centre but lacking the support of the right, could be invested only with the acquiescence of the communist party; and the approach of just such a prospect provoked the far right and the army into acting. On 13 May, a force of young settler extremists stormed and seized the main building of civil authority in Algiers, without interference from the armed police; paratroops took charge, and their commander, General Massu, proclaimed a joint civil and military Committee of Public Safety. A few hours later, a new government, under Pierre Pflimlin from a liberal limb of the Radicals, was approved by the National Assembly, with the communist deputies abstaining, to allow a large majority in the vote. But it soon became clear that this last guard of the old politics was without the will to withstand the assault from Algiers and the threat of civil war in France. With suitable encouragement from his immediate followers, who had worked so well both in Paris and Algiers to set the stage, General de

---

*Algerian nationalists maintained military bases in now independent Tunisia; and French forces in Algeria had been attacked near the frontier, allegedly by guerrillas from around the Tunisian village of Sakhiet. Much as the American army subsequently in Vietnam, the French in Algeria ascribed the elusiveness of victory in large part to the existence of enemy sanctuaries in neighbouring territories; and on his own initiative, General Salan, the Commander-in-Chief, sent twenty-five bombers to attack the supposed Sakhiet bases. Nothing of military value was apparently achieved; but seventy-five people, of whom some thirty were children attending the local school, were killed. Habib Bourguiba, the President of Tunisia, demanded the immediate withdrawal of all French troops stationed by previous agreement in the country, and the evacuation of the important French naval base at Bizerta. And the American government, which regarded the moderate Bourguiba regime as a bulwark against the spread of communism in the Arab world, intensified its efforts at promoting a settlement between French and Algerian nationalism.

Gaulle emerged from his retirement to rescue the state. He alone seemed able to command the confidence of the army, the support of the right and the reluctant collaboration of most in the broad distracted middle, who feared what might happen if he did not take command, more than what might happen if he did.* Receiving the investiture with special powers that he demanded from the National Assembly, he set about dismantling the Fourth Republic and constructing the presidential regime of the Fifth in its place.

It was ultimately the professional military who had provided him with power; and they had done so for their own purposes, not for his. Indeed, as he began perceptibly edging towards a deal with Algerian nationalism, it was again from Algiers that senior officers in the army, urged on by settler extremists, in 1960 and then yet more seriously in 1961, defied Paris. De Gaulle triumphed on both occasions; in part because he had, in varying measures of enthusiasm and acquiescence, the vast bulk of French public opinion behind him, so that he could summon to his defence the conscript ranks of the army itself; in part because he had the will decisively to employ the authority that this gave him, when even some of his own ministers were paralyzed by panic.

In short, he successfully confronted the threat of a neo-fascist military regime with his own grandiose brand of civil authoritarianism. For to describe his government as democratic, even by the common manipulative standards of liberal capitalism elsewhere, would be absurd. It was not, to be sure, the sort of 'fuehrer' rule of which his embittered demagogy in the late 'forties had given signs. He had apparently no longer the personal taste, or sense of political weakness, for the struttings and managed hysteria that had made the demonstrations of his RPF (Rally of the French People) then so nastily reminiscent. Yet his use of the referendum, by which the specific proposition was so phrased as to make acceptance all but certain, while the result would be assumed to convey a verdict on his general policies; his virtual monopoly of propaganda on radio and television; his establishment of an American executive authority, with the added power to dissolve a hostile legislature for new elections, and without the considerable prerogatives of constitutional check

*Thus, some half of the Socialist deputies voted for him.

enjoyed by the American judiciary; above all, his projection of himself as the sole alternative to social disaster: such constituted a regime that was, however popularly sanctioned it may have seemed, essentially Caesarian.

It was the defeat of an authoritarianism extrinsic to the system by an authoritarianism intrinsic to it. The Algerian settler leaders and their supporters in the French army command represented what had become a residual feudal morality, not unlike that of the slave-owners in the American South a century before: intolerable to the developed needs of capitalism in France. But in surmounting the challenge, the Gaullist regime itself represented not only the present triumph of liberal capitalism, but a prefiguration of the future terms on which the triumph would have to be sustained.

The essential achievement of the regime, indeed, was to fit France more firmly into the immediate development of the system, while in the process inevitably affecting this development as well. For, ironically, despite his dedication to the unique national role of France, as the effective suzerain of an independent European culture and force in the world, de Gaulle made his society not less American but more so. The formal empire was dissolved, except for a few tiny remnants, into separate independent states, secured for French ascendancy by bankers, industrialists, technicians, diplomats, military missions, trade agreements and loans, instead of by governors and armies: in a franc imitation of dollar imperialism. And within France itself, the social force of corporate business increased: as did, therefore, that of the mainly United States based giant multinational companies, for all the fulminations of the Gaullist regime against them.

The adroit financier and industrialist; the professional manager, the efficiency expert, the technician; the public relations officer, the salesman, the advertising agent; the bureaucrats of organized labour and of government itself: such were inheriting the earth ploughed by the periods of de Gaulle's historical mission. The successor to Notre Dame, Versailles, the tomb of Napoleon and the Eiffel Tower looked like becoming 'Le Drug-Store'. And when, in May 1968, there emerged the first real revolutionary challenge to capitalism in France, since the communist party had sold its birthright for a mess of institutional pottage, this started properly among the young, and especially the students; with the culture of competitive consumption as the new Bastille to be stormed.

The student population in France, though proportionately still small by American measure, had grown so rapidly – from 202,000 in 1961 to 514,000 in 1968[4] – that lecture halls, libraries, laboratories were overwhelmed; and any personal relationship between teacher and student had become American in its rareness. Functional university buildings were put up at ostentatious speed; but of a functionalism more appropriate to factory farming than to the nurture of the individual mind. The new campus at Nanterre, in the commuter belt of Paris, seemed to sum up much of what was wrong not only with French higher education, but with French society itself. There were no common rooms provided, and no cultural facilities. A huge swimming pool was rushed to completion, while the library building was left to lag behind. Sexually segregated residential quarters confronted each other across neuter territory. And the whole complex lay in a landscape of railway sidings, motorway construction, and low-cost monolithic blocks of flats mainly inhabited by immigrant labour. Furthermore, this was a campus for the Paris Faculties of Letters (which included Sociology) and of Law and Economics. Most of the over fifteen thousand students were of assured bourgeois background, with many from the fashionable enclosures of wealth in the capital. If large numbers of them were soon to give battle in the streets against the social order, this was not least because, like their American counterparts, they were finding in their own material prerogatives a moral ash.

In promoting both the articulate revolt and the widespread young disquiet on which this fed, the Vietnam war was a vital element. The de Gaulle regime, in seeking to assert the new role of French nationalism, expressed and encouraged distaste for the American engagement in Vietnam; so that the state television service transmitted frequent film, much of it from Hanoi, which did nothing to hide the horror of the war. Yet the interrelated operations of French and American capitalism continued: to become all the more evident by contrast. Antagonism among the young to the war increasingly saw in Gaullism an

71

intolerable hypocrisy, which displayed, in its very attempt to disguise, the coherent depravity of the system.

They were not, however, to be entrapped by the professional realism of conventional opposition politics. The crucially conservative attitude of the French communist party during the Algerian war had driven social disaffection then, into initiatives and organizations of its own. And now a seemingly similar stand by the party during the Vietnam war, with the far more searching moral discontent among the young, much advanced the process. For the spokesmen of a revolutionary commitment, who called for the victory of the Vietnamese National Liberation Front, the party slogan of 'Peace in Vietnam', scarcely distinguishable from the posture of Gaullism, highlighted the whole retreat of the French communist bureaucracy, as of the Soviet regime, from the cause of revolution. And, to be sure, was not the party employing the trade unions it controlled only to squeeze self-defeating material concessions from the property relations of capitalism: rather than to produce a basic change in property relations themselves? Was it not now openly in electoral alliance with the liberal rivals of de Gaulle? More and more it appeared an instrument of the system: indeed, a major factor in the resilient functioning of the bourgeois state. Associated in one or other specific Marxist ideological strain, in anarchism, or in some immediate coalition of revolutionary ideas, young militants set out to challenge the system on their own: in general with the hope that their challenge would precipitate, by example and by the repressive counter-measures of authority, a popular revolutionary endeavour. Such militants were collectively derided as the *enragés,* after the intransigent revolutionaries in the Paris Commune of 1793. They gladly adopted the name.

Nanterre was a centre of this militancy. And at the centre of the Nanterre militants was a young sociology student from West Germany, Daniel Cohn-Bendit, who brought, along with the ideas and techniques already developed by the *Sozialistischer Deutscher Studentenbund* (SDS), his personal brand of pert, irrepressible irreverence, to the conflict with authority. *Inorganisé et inorganisable,* he was complained of being, by his political colleagues.[5] But then, so, too, was the social challenge about to emerge. As event triggered event, what essentially occurred was an unorganized and unorganizable insurgency of the individual, in collective expression. And that is why there was no particular beginning; as there could be no end. Any recital of the nearest incidents must be arbitrary.

On 18 March 1968, the plate glass windows in the Paris branches of the Chase Manhattan Bank, the Bank of America, and Trans World Airlines, were shattered by explosives; and four days later, a group of *enragés* at Nanterre, protesting against the arrest of those held responsible for the explosions, occupied the administrative offices on the campus. From this demonstration came the Movement of 22 March, which determined to intensify harassment of the academic regime. By the night of 2 – 3 May, the regime had had enough: the Dean of Nanterre closed the Faculty of Letters until further notice; and Cohn-Bendit, with five other students, was summoned to appear before the University of Paris disciplinary council.

In the early afternoon of Friday 3 May, some five hundred students, including nearly all the leading militants, gathered in the central courtyard of the Sorbonne to protest. As the noisy meeting attracted a swelling student audience, the Rector consulted with the Minister of Education and authorized the entry of police to clear the courtyard. A contingent arrived and began arresting the demonstrators. The massed onlookers jeered, and chanted; someone threw a stone; and suddenly students were surging round the black police vans and blocking the road with a barricade of cars. The police replied with tear gas and with truncheons. Then, driven to frenzy by a barrage of stones, they burst through the Latin Quarter, felling bystanders and assailants alike. Men and women sitting at pavement cafés or reaching the streets from the Métro, suddenly found themselves being beaten or taken into custody. By evening, several hundred people had been injured, and some six hundred were under arrest.

With four young men sentenced to two months' imprisonment each; the Sorbonne closed by the Rector; and strikes or other demonstrations breaking out at provincial universities; some ten thousand marched, on Monday 6 May, in peaceful protest through the Latin Quarter. There were university teachers amongst them, and many teenage militants from the schools, mobilized by the *Comités d'Action Lycéens* which had come into being around the issue of the Vietnam war. A fierce police charge surprised them near the Sorbonne and again produced a battle in the streets, with hundreds of arrests. Social revolution was not yet in the air; and many of the bourgeoisie were far more alarmed at the treatment being meted out to their children by the forces of order, than at any perceptible threat to that order itself. On 8 May, a French public opinion poll (IFOP) reported support for the students from four out of every five Parisians. But the government of de Gaulle would not yield to the one student demand that might immediately have interrupted the gathering of revolt: the release and amnesty of student captives. Massive demonstrations, not only in the capital but in a dozen provincial towns, marked the progress of the week.

Then, on Friday 10 May, some five thousand teenagers from the schools met twice that number of students, to march in Paris for the freeing of their colleagues. Blocked by police in the Latin Quarter, they built barricades of overturned cars and piled-up cobble-stones.* The police summoned reinforcements; and in the early hours of 11 May, on government orders, launched an attack. As the battle raged, reports from radio stations beyond the control of the regime drew thousands of young Parisians, many of them workers, racing across the city, to support what now seemed like an uprising; while residents of the Quarter, stirred by the savagery of the police, gave help and refuge to the injured and fleeing. At half-past five in the morning, with a broadcast by Cohn-Bendit, protesters who had become insurgents, began dispersing from that particular battlefield. At five, students in Strasbourg, who had been following events on their radios, took possession of their university and proclaimed its autonomy.

That Saturday night, prime minister Georges Pompidou, on his return from abroad, announced the reopening of the Sorbonne and implied that imprisoned students would be released. It was too late. The students were not to be thus conciliated now. And others had glimpsed the opportunity. The country's two main trade union federations, including the communist party controlled CGT (*Confédération Générale du Travail*), had joined the leading organization of teachers, in

*The *pavé*, cubic and weighing some three pounds, that is the material of so many French streets, and proved so effective a missile as well.

calling for mass strikes and demonstrations on 13 May: the tenth anniversary of the putsch in Algiers which had brought de Gaulle to power. But appropriately, in the march of eight hundred thousand that took place in Paris on that day, the foremost student militants were in front; with the trade union bosses behind; and still further back, the politicians of the communist party and their competitors in the constitutional left. With the conclusion of the march, students swept on to the Sorbonne and occupied it. And across France universities were seized by their students.

For a while, the young imagination seemed to dance on the moral grave of the system. On the walls across Paris, within the university buildings and without, a generation scrawled spontaneous witnesses to its insurgent faith. *Le rêve est réalité* – the dream is reality. *Interdire d'interdire* – it is forbidden to forbid. *L'Etat c'est chacun de nous* – the state is each of us. *Soyez réalistes, demandez l'impossible* – be realists, demand the impossible. *L'anarchie c'est je* – anarchy is I. *L'agresseur n'est pas celui qui se révolte mais celui qui affirme* – the aggressor is not he who revolts but he who maintains. *Un homme n'est pas stupide ou intelligent: il est libre ou il n'est pas* – a man is not stupid or clever: he is free or he is not. *Une révolution qui demande que l'on se sacrifie pour elle est une révolution à la papa* – a revolution that requires you to sacrifice yourself for it, is a revolution that belongs to daddy. *Dessous les pavés c'est la plage* . . . . Beneath the cobble-stones is the beach. . . .[6]

From the occupied Ecole Nationale des Beaux-Arts issued a cascade of brilliant posters, their designs adopted by a school assembly of students and teachers, to bear the revolutionary message through the Paris streets. The latest tracts, journals, cartoons circulated among eager pavement crowds. Hurrying passers-by stopped for a moment to watch, and stayed to listen and discuss. The Sorbonne itself, proclaimed by its occupants an autonomous popular university, was open night and day; and if workers did not arrive in the multitudes hoped, individual Parisians of all classes came, to go away deriding, mystified, or with their minds excited to new possibilities. In the courtyard were flags and portraits and music; and in dozens of upstairs rooms, students along with sympathetic teachers and visitors thought and talked together of what education, and of what society should be about.* The new mood invaded and seized long-comatose faculties, specialist schools, even theological seminaries, across Paris and the provinces. It reached through the *lycées*, drawing teenagers by the tens of thousands into a social awareness and moral scrutiny. Doctors, lawyers, architects, actors, painters, musicians, journalists, broadcasters began to examine the structure and functioning of their respective professions, and to demand radical changes.

But it was the response of labour that looked suddenly like turning a student revolt into social revolution. Fired by the university occupations, workers began to down tools and take over their factories. On 14 May, no more than a few hundred were on strike. By 22 May, the number exceeded nine million. And the spread, as the initiative, was spontaneous. At no time did the various trade union federations, and in particular the predominant CGT, order or organize such action. Indeed, the communist command of the CGT was manifestly alarmed by a momentum that threatened to dismantle its own institutional control of labour; to promote the influence of Trotskyists, Maoists and yet more dangerously unidentifiable heretics of revolutionary adventurism; and to produce a confrontation with the social order that might calamitously fail, or calamitously succeed. It instructed its local officials to do what they could to prevent students from entering the factories, and hastened to seek quick concessions for labour from the vulnerability of the government.

And the government seemed increasingly vulnerable. De Gaulle's address to the nation on 24 May, proposing a referendum for a 'mandate of renewal', and promising reforms of an unpersuasive elusiveness, disheartened his supporters, as it invigorated the challenge to his regime, and beyond that, the challenge to the social order itself. Violence flared, and young workers demonstrated with banners proclaiming 'Power for the workers!' 'Power is in the street!' On the following day, Georges Séguy, secretary-general of the CGT, alongside other labour bosses, sat down at the Ministry of Social Affairs, for talks with

*There was also, of course, some dangerous silliness, as with the burning of books. But no one who witnessed the engagement to cultural liberation could reasonably have seen such excesses as central. The force of a revolutionary current is bound to stir up mental mud. It is when the mud chokes the very current that revolution repudiates itself.

officials of the main employer organizations, and with government representatives led by prime minister Pompidou. By the morning of Monday 27 May, an agreement had been reached which yielded substantially higher wages, with a list of further improvements in conditions of work. Séguy had, shortly before, described his union as *'la grande force tranquille'*.

But from factories across the country came protests at the agreement. And Séguy himself, reporting his victory to twenty-five thousand Renault workers, was received with catcalls. 'Revolution today *is* possible', André Barjonet, who had resigned as economic adviser to the CGT, declared to a mass meeting in Paris, called by the national union of students (UNEF) and attended by thousands of militant young workers as well. But it was the counter-attack by authority that succeeded. While the leading politicians of the constitutional left manoeuvred for advantage in securing what now seemed the easy spoils of the Fifth Republic, with the communist party intent on getting a suitable share, de Gaulle prepared to fight.* Leaving Paris, he met various army commanders† and was assured of their assistance should he need to invoke it. On Thursday afternoon, 30 May, in the capital again, he addressed the nation. He would not resign. He would defer the referendum. He would dissolve the National Assembly for general elections. There was an attempt to impose a communist dictatorship, and he would resist it. Civic action in defence of the republic should be taken 'everywhere and at once'. And he announced his readiness to use 'other means', should these prove necessary.

Gaullist organizers had not been idle in the hours before, and some million supporters poured through the streets of Paris to affirm their loyalty at the Etoile. *'Le communisme ne passera pas'*, they chanted; and, sporadically, *'Cohn-Bendit à Dachau!'* Para-military committees in defence of the republic sprang up across the country. The government began calling out skilled reservists to man essential services. And in the early hours of Friday morning, as an opening shot, armed police expelled workers picketing the central post office in Rouen. The communist party, faced with the alternative of backing a revolution-

---

*His will stiffened, it was widely reported at the time, by Pompidou.

†Aptly including General Massu, who was now commander of the French forces stationed in West Germany.

ary endeavour which it had discouraged and now more than ever feared, flung itself into the electoral campaign. Most factories would stay occupied until well into June; and often be surrendered only after wage increases still higher than those negotiated by the trade unions in May. But the movement of industrial defiance began clearly to crumble. On 12 June, the government outlawed various organizations of the revolutionary left that had been prominent in the student revolt: to temperate protests from the communist party.

At the polls – on 23 and 30 June – the parties of the constitutional left suffered the most severe collective electoral reverse in their history: while the Gaullists, having composed themselves for the occasion into the Union for the Defence of the Republic, won an overall majority at last. No more than 42.6 per cent of the voters supported parties of the constitutional left, in contrast with the sixty-five per cent straight after the Second World War. And the representation of the communist party itself was more than halved: from seventy-three to thirty-four seats. Ten days later, de Gaulle dismissed Pompidou, who had master-minded the Gaullist electoral campaign, as prime minister. But this did not alter the fact that the authoritarian security of the social order appeared no longer dependent upon the person of de Gaulle.

Nowhere and at no time under liberal capitalism has the system seemed so close to being overthrown as it did in France during a few days of 1968. Yet to see how and why it survived is to see also how and why its success must be accounted as no more than a stage in its cumulative failure. It may well be that for those who took the initiative in industrial defiance, the impulse was a deep discontent with the nature of the system. It was, significantly, the younger workers who first responded to the university occupations. Some of them had already joined in student-led street demonstrations; and if they had not been such before, they had become insurgents in the process. In many worker-occupied factory yards, straw-filled dummies, labelled 'capitalism', were suspended from makeshift gallows. But the vast majority of those who followed the initiative, were more discontented with their place in the system than with the system itself. They were plainly fed up with a government that had been there so complacently for so long, pursuing grandiose policies at their expense. Certainly, the bourgeoisie showed scant signs of engaging in austerity. Competitive consumption was all too conspicuous, and made the material denials felt by workers accordingly the more provocative. Gaullist self-gratulation at the huge accumulated gold reserves with which to teach the dollar a lesson, became a mounting affront. If any increase in earnings was so often so soon overtaken by material inflation, still less could it keep pace with the moral inflationary rate of prosperity with glory. Once the student revolt had detonated a response on some factory floor, the mass of workers were quick to see the possibilities presented. And once aware of the power that the extent of their defiance had attained, they were not to be bought off by concessions that trade unions leaders, who had so manifestly failed to lead before, now wrested so easily from the government. But when it came to an ultimate trial of strength with the social order, they were neither prepared nor willing. The immediate rewards of their militancy were not to be put at risk in a struggle for some untried system, that might suit them rather less than the one they had.

Of course the communist party, with its CGT the strongest organized force among French workers, was responsible for blunting the revolutionary edge of events. From the outset, it was unequivocal in its opposition to confronting capitalism; and as industrial defiance spread despite its efforts, it hastened to make the best bargain that it could, to draw back labour and government from a collision over the social order itself. Yet, surely, to say, as so many in the revolutionary left have since said, that the French communist party betrayed the French workers in 1968, is both to conceal and reveal the truth at once. The French workers were betrayed because they betrayed themselves. Indeed, if the French communist party had become a bureaucratic institution, intent on the climb to constitutional power and essentially in service to the bourgeois state, this was, in undeniable part, because it had accepted the psychical engagement of French workers to capitalism. It led as it followed. And the result was a vicious circle of accommodation. The more that the communist party acted in the belief that French workers were fundamentally committed to the system, the more committed, under the influence of the communist party, French workers seemed fundamentally to be; and the more committed to the system French workers seemed fundamentally to be, the more the communist party acted in this belief. If revolution was, after all, not possible in 1968, it was because most French workers and the French communist party had persuaded each other so. And they had persuaded each other so, ultimately because neither wanted revolution. Both saw themselves as likely to lose more than they would gain.

But none of this should suggest that revolution was there simply for the taking. The challenge to the system was defeated not least because it was seen at last, however distortedly, as that. While no more than the policies of the government, or even its particular survival, appeared under assault from students, a sizable sector of French society, including an important number of the bourgeoisie, sympathized with the assailants. Massive industrial defiance dissipated much of the sympathy, but kept the engagement to one over the future of Gaullism. It was de Gaulle himself, by treating the industrial defiance as the revolutionary endeavour it was not, who made the danger to his government the occasion for a social duel over the future of capitalism itself. By raising the bugbear of a communist plot to seize power, he virtually ensured his constitutional triumph within the system. And by brandishing the threat of the army to protect constitutional authority, he made revolution the only alternative to acquiescence. His confidence trick gave him the best of both worlds. The one opposition force with the organized base to provide this social duel with sufficient immediate substance, was a communist party now more than ever committed against any such eventuality: yet it was de Gaulle's projected commitment of the communist party to just such an eventuality which enabled him to represent the cause of his government as the cause of the system. The real revolutionaries, among the students and the younger workers, did not stand a chance. Caught between a communist party which, with other constituents of the constitutional left, laboured to escape the electoral embarrassment of any association with revolutionary aims and activities; and a government which, with its self-assurance more than restored, now increasingly employed the repressive power of the state: they were isolated into dying outbursts of rage and recrimination.

Yet society will not, cannot be again what it was. The

challenge to the system may not have gained the state; but it gained a multitude of minds. Indifference became disquiet, and disquiet, disaffection, for thousands of students, whose imagination was awakened to a new sense of personal and social purpose. Few who took part in the street battles with the police will forget the face of order that they encountered; as few who took part in the university occupations will forget the beach that each in his own way saw gleaming beneath the stones. And the experience reached far into the schools, so that thousands still to enter the universities will arrive already stirred by insurgent ideas. Furthermore, though the course of industrial defiance scarcely corroborated student faith in the revolutionary promise of labour, it revealed disillusionment enough among younger workers with the functioning of the system and a readiness to confront the bureaucratic institutions claiming to represent them. If, like the students, such younger workers as well failed to rouse those elusive masses to revolution, they roused themselves; and it is all too probable that, like the students, with whom some of them established a communion in idealism, they will see their defeat as their vital rights denied.

For them, too, there had been gleams of the beach beneath the stones. In Nantes, where the first of the factory occupations occurred, on 14 May, at the nearby Sud-Aviation aircraft plant, students already on strike at the university rushed to the aid of workers with money and blankets and reinforcements for the picket lines. Despite the attitude adopted at their national headquarters, the local trade union officials welcomed this collaboration; and a Central Strike Committee was formed, with representatives of the three big industrial unions; of the militant student and teacher unions*; and even of two agricultural unions.† Road blocks cut off the town from all traffic unauthorized by the Committee, which issued its own petrol coupons and travel permits for the supply of necessities to the farms and the occupied factories, and which opened six retail trade outlets in local schools. Workers and students went to help in the fields, and the flow of food to the town was not interrupted. Indeed, far from

---

*UNEF, or *Union National des Etudiants de France*: and FEN, or *Fédération de l'Education Nationale*.

†FNSEA, or *Fédération Nationale des Syndicats d'Exploitants Agricoles;*[8] and CNJA, or *Centre National des Jeunes Agriculteurs*.

the leap in prices that might have been expected, the elimination of middleman profit produced a substantial fall; while families to whose formidable poverty this made little difference, were assisted by the issue of food chits. Nantes had traditionally been a centre of division between worker and peasant, with the propertied order able to rely upon the allegiance of the countryside. Yet here at last peasants and workers were moving together, along with teachers, students, and pupils from the *lycées,* in an exploration of popular government. It was an experiment that lasted in body hardly more than two weeks, from the middle of May to the beginning of June, when the road-blocks were dismantled under threat of armed convoys from Paris. It is unlikely so to have passed from the minds of those who knew themselves, as never before, personally alive, and collectively creative, because of it.

But any social analysis that, in identifying categories of experience and attitude, seeks to dispossess the individual, contradicts its purpose. It ceases accordingly to be about people, and denies as it demonstrates. True, certain students, teachers, workers, peasants, significantly as such, associated themselves with, and were profoundly changed by, the revolutionary challenge of 1968. But so affecting and affected, too, was this or that person, from a peculiarly hostile social category. '*Parlez à vos voisins*' (talk to your neighbours) was among the messages on a wall of the Sorbonne annexe in the rue de Censier. And in that tumultuous May, people talked and began to reach each other, as they had not before been able or willing to do. For of all the treasons to the cause of capitalism, this is the highest: that people should search and find one another, without property coming in between. And how should the impact of this engagement in personality be exaggerated?

The revolutionary challenge was defeated, to be sure. But no victory is more dangerous than the one which can neither eliminate nor accommodate the defeated. In the end it is itself a defeat. The system by its triumph only intensified the dedication of its enemies; their sense of inevitable outrage at its hands; their rejection of all that it had, for them so destructively, to offer. Of relevance, the constituency with the leading abstention rate in the elections – 35.6 per cent – was the student strong-hold of the Paris Latin Quarter. And the electoral roll, with a third of the inscribed over fifty-five years old, scarcely favoured the representation of youth. Since then, there has been sporadic challenge in the form of industrial sabotage, arson, and other attacks on property. Yes, of course, the system has the means to shake off such material damage. But what it cannot shake off is the moral damage, that it must do to itself, in its essentially repressive response.*

To call the present an age of revolutions is to call it, too, an age of counter-revolutions. But the second must clear, in its very attempt to block, the way for the first. Amid all the reasons for the defeat of slavery in the American South, momentously must be numbered the hysteria of a regime which felt itself trapped by time: driven, by the sense of its increasing vulnerability, to pre-empt the initiative in civil war, and so provoke a defeat that it might, simply by waiting, for who knows how much longer still have avoided. Just when and how the social order of Russia would fundamentally have changed, had the Tsarist regime conducted itself differently, is a diverting speculation. What is pertinent, is that the peculiar mixture of arrogant and uneasy absolutism which was the regime of

*Within a year, de Gaulle himself was to resign, after marginal defeat in a referendum on senate and regional reform; and Pompidou was elected president to succeed him. The system seemed to have found a rather more representative figure in the former banker, with an apparent aptitude for manipulative politics and in particular the conciliation of labour bosses. Yet, paradoxically, the popular base of Pompidou was much narrower. At the presidential heat of 1 June 1969, he received 44.46 per cent of the vote: to 23.31 per cent for Alain Poher, candidate of the centre; 21.28 per cent for Jaques Duclos of the communist party; and a remainder almost equally divided between Gaston Defferre of the socialists, and the total for Trotskyist and radical socialist candidates. But the abstentions and spoilt ballots, in contrast with previous comparable performances at the national polls, reached almost 23 per cent. And in the presidential final between Pompidou and Poher on 15 June, with the communist party having called for a boycott, the sum of abstentions and spoilt ballots rose to over 35 per cent of the registered electorate. No more than 37 per cent of the country's voters placed Pompidou in office: representing a manifest shift in the command of constitutional power to the resurgent right, with a strong element, as the electoral campaign had indicated, of authoritarian idealism. Even in 1965, with his support seriously diminished, de Gaulle had won 55 per cent of the vote in a final poll of some 82.5 per cent, after spoilt ballots were added to abstentions: collecting two million more votes, from an electorate smaller by half-a-million, than Pompidou would do four years later.

Nicholas II, did much, by its own agressions, to promote its overthrow. But could it, in fact, have been otherwise? Or did each such regime, given its moral obsolescence, not have to behave as it did? A social system ascendant, self-assured in its virtual monopoly of idealism, is itself its major source of strength. Confronted by the new idealism that its ascendancy has engendered, it becomes itself its major source of weakness.

The most obvious challenge is the challenge of violence: the unlawful exercise of force. Yet the challenge of violence is precisely the challenge of law. The body of enacted or customary rules recognized by the community as binding, ceases to be recognized by a growing number of citizens as reasonable and just; ceases accordingly to be recognized by them as binding, and becomes for them intolerable instead. They make their own law, in keeping with the moral antithesis that informs their disaffection, and see the social system itself as essentially violent; as unlawfully exercising force by the very nature of its dominion. With its moral premises less and less able to ensure sufficient acquiescence in its functioning, the system more and more depends on force, to secure the established order, for being order; the established law, for being the law.

Indeed, how else can a liberal capitalism so confronted, protect itself, except by increasingly revealing itself as the very violence that those revolting against it claim it to be? Increasingly it must resort to coercive means that contradict the pretensions to personal freedom which have commanded its moral support. Increasingly it must sacrifice life to the cause of property. Increasingly it must demonstrate a corporate despotism over the individual. Its collapse, however delayed, is inescapable.

No system can indefinitely survive on overt repression. Yet no system can survive without overt repression unless it is morally inclusive. Once liberal capitalism is seen, and correspondingly treated by sufficient of its citizens* as inevitably excluding their individual sense of purpose, the police and the soldiers must come from behind as the source of authority. A system always covertly repressive becomes overtly so. The call to rev-

*What constitutes 'sufficient', lies in the event. But certainly an effectual minority does not need to be large. The tiny Front for the Liberation of Quebec, by kidnapping and killing one prominent politician, provoked the Liberal government of Canada into declaring a national state of emergency, with the suspension of normal civil rights by martial law.

olution makes the menaced social order counter-revolutionary: in a reinforcement of denial that can only promote revolution. In short, by acting to protect itself against the challenge from the idealism of personality, liberal capitalism must become something differently the same: the reasserted moral thesis of property in the final form of fascism.*

And this process, it must be stressed, is not solely to be associated with the authoritarian momentum of the convention- ally identified right. For, to discern the dynamic of the system only in the developing organizations of capital, and not in those of labour, is to mistake the proper function of the social democratic left: with the structure and role of the trade unions, and of the constitutional parties with which they are connected. This movement is crucial to liberal capitalism. Its distinctiveness is one of emphasis: to temper and so assure the competitive re- lationships of the market. It cannot save the system from fascism: it can merely promote, with its peculiar preoccupations and techniques, its own variant.† Its engagement to the priorities of property must require, more and more forcibly as this is resisted, the submission of the individual to its own corporate undertakings. Its prescriptions may well appear materi- ally beneficial for the mass of citizens; may perhaps for a while appear to confer commensurate moral benefits: but it is ultimately at least as destructive of the individual; and it will, it must respond to the idealism that assails its law, at least as violently with the resources of the state.

George Orwell, who in his total commitment to the priorities of personality belongs to the true moral lineage of the revolution- ary left, was tormented by just this vision in writing *1984*. He named his system of perfected fascism 'Ingsoc' or English Social-

---

*Fascism is strictly the form of nationalist, anti-communist corporate politics of the Mussolini era in Italy, which was imitated, with variations, in other countries. But it has come to mean the supremely authoritarian society in which the regime seeks to suppress all dissent, and treats all citizens as mere constituents of particular corporate entities: to secure, if by accordingly qualifying, the power of property. And what more useful term exists for the essential counter-revolutionary state, towards which liberal capitalist society is moving?

†It was, thus, the Labour government of Harold Wilson (1964–70) which initia- ted the present attempts in Britain to place labour under more effective corporate control.

ism;* and his hero, the lonely man to stand out, in vain, against it, Winston Smith, after Winston Churchill, surely one of the most recalcitrant figures on the conventional right in modern English history. But, of course, *1984* itself is, in its very despair, incompatible with the idealism of the revolutionary left; as it is incompatible too, with the nature of the very system whose totalitarian promise he saw. It came from an imagination crippled by the sheer weight of physical and moral distress. For the world of *1984* works, and can only work, through a retreat from the priorities of property; while the fascist momentum of liberal capitalism, including that of its constituent left, lies not in the relative denial of such priorities, but rather in the blind devotion to them. To see the consummation of the system as the pursuit of corporate power through a state in mass material decay, is socially untenable. Such a development would be interrupted soon enough, whatever the excuses of occasion, by the popular force that supplies the system with its decisive following, in the bulk of labour. If so many people have proved deludable by material bribes, it is by material bribes that they have been deluded. Indeed, the survival of the system, and certainly not least in its final refuge of fascism, lies precisely in its continuing capacity to provide such material bribes.

Yet this is at the same time its peril. For in preserving its capacity to provide material bribes, it must promote the very social elements which revolt against its purposes. It does not now spend more and more on higher education, for instance, to indulge the personal whims of some among its youth. It does so in part because enough citizens expect and require increasing opportunities for their children to reach university; but also because the system, for its own prosperity, needs the skills which higher education supplies. To threaten, therefore, as do the more frantic adherents of the counter-revolutionary commitment, that

*Many of the techniques practised by his regime were projected from those already to be found in the Soviet Union of Stalin and the subservient communist parties of the West. And, indeed, the term 'fascism' to describe the essential counter-revolutionary system, may no less justly be applied where the power of property, corporately served, belongs to the state, than where it belongs to the private citizen. Such a system remains, whatever its political vocabulary and pretensions, fundamentally anti-communist: or fundamentally hostile to what revolutionary socialism should be about. But that Orwell did not see *1984* as the mere world triumph of Soviet fascism is, surely, clear by his particular employment of 'Ingsoc', in a fantasy of institutionalized power bloc struggle.

society may be driven to keep the number of students at the present level, or even reduce it, is to threaten that increasingly illness will have to go untreated by doctors; criminal proceedings undefended, and corporate business unattended by lawyers; science and industry unsustained, let alone advanced, by researchers and technicians. No surer way of frustrating that rise in accepted standards of material welfare, on which popular acquiescence in the system essentially rests, than deliberately stunting the development and acquisition of urgent skills, can scarcely be visualized.

An alternative proposal is to eliminate trouble-makers on the campus by withdrawing their grants or expelling them. But as events on one troubled campus after another have revealed, students react against such particular chastisements with an insurgent sense of their collective identity. If one set of declared trouble-makers is removed, is another, yet larger, not likely to take its place? And where is the purging to stop? Moreover, in a representative dilemma of the system, there has been a clearly demonstrable correspondence between academic achievement and initiative in revolt.* If those with apparently the keenest intellects, by the appreciations of the system itself, are, for their related revolt, to be dismissed from their studies, the standards of higher education, and hence the quality of the skills that the system needs to supply, can hardly be prevented from deteriorating.

But then material bribery itself must prove counter-productive. For if from among this generation of youth, materially the best served, by traditional definition, in history, so many should have reacted not with invigorated greed and acquiescence, but with such antagonism to the system responsible, it is not sensibly to be believed that its successors will react all that differently. And the process must, in some measure, be cumulative. Students do graduate and themselves gain offices of authority, and young workers become older ones; discarding earlier perceptions and commitments along the way. But it is, surely, improbable that its peculiar perceptions and commitments, with the tracks of the experience that gave these such momentous life, should alto-

---

*At the London School of Economics or Nanterre, as at Berkeley or Harvard, the holders of fellowships or other academic awards have usually been in the forefront of the challenge to authority.

gether disappear from this generation. The challenge to the system must come not only from its immediate young, but from more and more of those who were its young before and whose imagination, once awakened, has withstood being put back to sleep.

And, above all, the system must, in becoming more and more manifestly repressive as it seeks to resist the revolutionary claims of personality, raise against itself those who are not necessarily from this or that, then or now, peculiarly disaffected social element, but from this or that person who knows his very meaning to be violated; his proper purpose defied.

No less is, of course, in its own way true of the Soviet system; where even aside from the crude imperial aspects of Soviet rule, there is, in the proclaimed socialist homeland itself, more than enough to provoke a revolutionary idealism. Over half a century since the revolution of 1917, liberty, equality, fraternity, the cardinal values of socialism, are a mockery and a rebuke : when not, in various attempts to express them, tried and punished as crimes against the state. Economic discrepancies are everywhere evident : between city and countryside – between advanced and backward regions; above all, between one person and another, according to the price tag on his social function. The existence of an elite, with standards of consumption towering above those of the multitude, is beyond denial, if not the dogmas of an intricate sophistry.

'Oh! Come off it, father!' [cries Clara to Major-General Pyotre Makarygin, State Prosecutor, in Alexander Solzhenitsyn's novel, *The First Circle*.] 'You don't belong to the working class. You were a worker once for two years and you've been a prosecutor for thirty. You – a worker! You live off the fat of the land! You even have a chauffeur to drive your own car! Environment determines consciousness – isn't that what your generation taught us?'

'*Social* environment, you idiot! And *social* consciousness!'

'What is that? Some people have mansions and others sheds, some have cars and others have holes in their shoes.

What's social about it?'

'You're stupid.... You don't understand anything and you won't learn....'

'Go on then, teach me! Go on! Where does all your salary come from? Why do they pay you thousands of roubles when you don't produce anything?'

'*Accumulated* labour, you fool! Read Marx! Education, special training – that's accumulated labour, you're paid more for it. Why d'you think they pay you eighteen hundred at your research institute?'[7]

Yet if the Claras, in fiction and doubtless in fact, can safely so assail the system within the privacies of privilege, public assaults in general prove a great deal more costly. Protesting intellectuals without adequate protection are subjected to show trials and severe penalties. For sufficient display is needed to confront the force of example. And other representatives of a displeasing collective identity or social trend, not always chosen for their personal responsibility, are similarly disciplined. In particular, the regime sporadically singles out Jews for judgement, to reveal that it has learnt and forgotten little since this technique was employed by its Tsarist predecessors.

But who can know how many individual citizens, at almost all levels of society, suffer concealed chastisement of one sort or another, for some semblance of disloyalty? What is certain is that there are those who, by their office, and in the name of protecting party and state, enjoy lavish power over the lives of others; that this power, without popular accountability, is often secretly, and even when openly, arbitrarily employed; and that abuses of its professed social purposes are, therefore, rife. Indeed, there can be few constitutional governments outside the Soviet system where the constitutions themselves are so elaborate with the recital of rights possessed by the individual citizen, and where in practice such assurances count for quite so little. In effect, the bureaucracy is the law; and the only rule of law is the rule of bureaucratic process. Since the ultimate allegiance of any bureaucracy is to its own survival, and since this survival can only be endangered by belief in their fallibility, bureaucrats themselves, except to higher bureaucrats, make no mistakes: or, at least, make them only long after they have made them, when the defects have been corrected by internal discipline, and infallibility is once more restored.

But to admit previous fallibility, whatever the consequent corrections, is to imply the possibilities of fallibility again. And, paradoxically, though civil decencies are much less capriciously and contemptuously violated now than they were under the leadership of Stalin, the public pronouncement of Stalinist error has made their violation correspondingly less tolerable. To many loyal subjects of the system, the revelations at the Twentieth Congress of the Soviet Party, and ensuing revelations by authority across the empire, came as a moral shock from which their confidence has never recovered.* Wrongs done by a system which could do no wrong, were too often not seen as such. Wrongs done by a system which has admitted to having done wrong at all – let alone wrong of the magnitude that has officially been attributed to Stalin – are more likely so to be seen, with disturbing inferences drawn.

And if liberty, equality, fraternity are socialist values that the system has more and more manifestly failed to provide, more and more manifest, too, is its failure to provide the sufficient growth in material product that was to promote such values, and make liberal capitalism appear an ineffectual anachronism by contrast. No longer heard are such claims as issued proudly from the Khrushchev leadership at the start of the 'sixties : that the Soviet Union would soon outstrip the United States in national product, and by 1980 reach a stage of material abundance to allow the experiment of true communism at last, with the principle applied of 'each according to his needs'. Indeed, economic developments at the half-way mark of 1970 indicated mounting difficulties. And a quarter of a century afterwards, the devastations of the Second World War could not furnish the explanation and excuse that they had done. It was all too significant that in the signing of a non-aggression treaty between the Soviet Union and the Federal German Republic in August 1970, the prospect of capital loans and technical assistance from the second should have been a notable inducement for the first.

The indictment, like the warning, contained in a letter to the

*If many such revelations have been made only to selected audiences, their content has been carried far beyond by uncontrollable report, and by deductions from what is publicly admitted.

leadership of the Soviet bureaucracy, from three Soviet intellectuals – academician Andre Sakharov, celebrated for his work on the hydrogen bomb; historian Roy Medvedev; and physicist Valentin Tourchine – was serious enough.[8] In comparing the Soviet economy with that of the United States, they declared that 'we are behind not only quantitatively, but also – saddest to say – qualitatively. . . . We are, simply, living in another era'. The real income of the Soviet people had in recent years only with difficulty been raised, and there were clear signs of inflation. Even Soviet educational standards, long the especial pride and promise of the system, were not spared. 'The slackening in the development of education is particularly disquieting for the future of our country. In fact, our total outlays on education are less than those of the United States and rising at a slower rate.' Nor did the condition of science and technology give more comfort. 'The second industrial revolution has begun, and now, at the start of the 'seventies, we can see that not only have we not overtaken America, but the gap between our two countries is widening.'

The three critics laid the blame carefully not on 'socialist structures', but on 'anti-democratic traditions' and a conduct of public affairs 'hostile to socialism'. The 'problems of organization and management . . . cannot be resolved by one man or several who dispose of power and possess a ubiquitous knowledge'. The necessary economic measures depended upon wider reform. 'A scientific approach demands complete information, impartial thought, and the freedom to create. While these conditions do not exist (and not only for some people, but for the mass), to speak of scientific management will be nothing but words.' At present, there existed instead, reciprocal mistrust and 'a total absence of mutual comprehension'. What justification could there be for 'the confinement in prison, in camps or in mental hospitals, of people whose opposition stays within the framework of the law, within the domain of ideas and convictions?'

The letter called for a programme of change, 'within the next four or five years', to include: a statement by the highest authorities of the party and the government on the need for greater 'democratization'; the 'diffusion, at first restricted, then gradually generalized, of information on the state of the country and on problems of public interest'; the diffusion, as well, of information on the outside world, through freedom to hear foreign radio transmissions, the introduction of foreign publications, and the extension of tourism; the establishment of an institute 'for the study of public opinion'; the 'organization of industrial associations endowed with a high degree of independence'; the amnesty of political prisoners and the publication of their trial records; and the more open election of candidates to 'the organs of the party and to the soviets'.* The 'democratization' of Soviet society could bring to birth 'an enthusiasm comparable to that at the beginning of the 'twenties'. Failure to undertake such a process would risk transforming the country into 'a provincial power of the second rank'. The warning was urgent. 'Today, it is possible for us to take the right road and realize the necessary reforms. In a few years perhaps, it will be too late.'

According to Semionov, the Soviet sociologist, the intelligentsia of the Soviet Union has three main constituents: 'the higher officials in the political and economic administration of the state (between 2.4 and three million people); the technical and economic intelligentsia (between five and six millions); and the scientific and cultural intelligentsia (between 5.3 and six millions).'† It would be far from surprising if more and more in these last two groups, and even among the less near-sighted and securely situated in the first, were to resent the restrictions so arbitrarily imposed on their activities and very ideas. Indeed, it is reasonable to see in this sector a middle class of relative privilege and relative deprivation, of frustration and fear, such as fired struggle so often in the past against an obsolescent regime. And to be sure, the ends and means suggested in the letter from the three intellectuals seem informed more by what liberal capitalism already offers, than by what a genuine socialism would offer instead. Pertinently, the three give scant attention to ultimate social problems, but content themselves with the remark: 'It is clear that this programme must be completed by a plan of econo-

* The soviets are the elected councils of government in the Soviet Union. But their subservience to the bureaucracy is demonstrated by the recommendation in the letter that greater responsibility should be granted to the local, regional and central ones.

† Semionov excludes from his estimate those 'higher officials' without university education.

mic and social measures elaborated by specialists.' And pertinently, too, nationalism, so common an engagement of the
middle class in history, is no trifling factor in their anxious
initiative. Calling in evidence 'the danger of totalitarian Chinese
nationalism' – as though evidence for the danger of totalitarian
Soviet nationalism did not exist – they pronounced the need to
maintain, if not increase, 'the economic and technological gap
between our country and China'. So much for world brotherhood
in revolution.

The three intellectuals seem as remote from the mass of
Soviet peasants and workers as the very bureaucracy they
criticize. But however their impulse and remedies may be
regarded, their alarm is abundantly justified by the social
predicament.[9] Despite reforms bringing agricultural labour at
last to the same level of guaranteed minimum wage and basic
social security provisions as that for industrial workers, and
despite agricultural investments that now account for some
twenty per cent of the annual Soviet budget, the countryside has
displayed a distressing reluctance to meet the requirements of the
state. Peasants continue to give as little time as possible to the
interests of their collective farms. According to official Soviet
statistics, a peasant in the Ukraine, the national granary, works
only an average 180 days a year for his collective farm; and in
Georgia, for all the mildness of the climate, only 135: his
private plot absorbs the rest of his efforts. The development of
Siberia and the Soviet Far East, a policy bespoke for economic
rescue, and made the more urgent by the quarrel with China, is
failing. Despite such inducements as subsidies in kind, substantially higher wages and longer holidays, for labour to migrate
there, the population of these areas has actually declined rather
than risen in the past four years.

Industrial reforms, such as somewhat more autonomy in the
management of individual enterprises, to encourage competition
in attracting labour and so promote efficiency, have had, it
seems, unfortunate effects. The rival allurement of higher wages
has led to an enormous internal migration of workers, with
enterprises in certain industries experiencing a virtually complete change of labour force within the space of three years. And
according to Soviet estimates, a worker moving from one
enterprise to another loses, on average, a month of productive

work; or more than two months, when changing his locality as well. Nor, despite the enormous capital sums spent on modernizing industry, does the wasteful use of unskilled labour seem to have been significantly reduced. Soviet statistics reveal that one worker out of three is occupied in loading or transporting goods: whereas, in the United States, twenty-five or twenty-six workers are engaged in production, for every one engaged in the transport process. Even in wholly new factories bought from abroad, productivity is far lower than in their foreign prototypes: with as many as eight times the number of workers employed, to achieve the same output. The Soviet press itself all too frequently complains of how rarely the modernization of old plant leads to the more efficient use of labour. There are instances, indeed, where such modernization appears to have produced no decrease at all, or even an increase, in the work force.

One reason for this may be, as Karol suggests, the activity of the trade unions, which make up for their docility towards problems of production, as towards the wider social problems, by a diligent concern with security of employment. Another may be the practised timidity of management, which resists appeals from the central planning authorities for the collaboration of individual enterprises, and prefers to ensure its supplies by manufacturing as many of them as possible in its own workshops. Such industrial annexes are obviously less efficient than specialized factories, and absorb a multitude of workers who might otherwise be far more productive. Together with the drying up of the surplus labour supply from the countryside, the rapid growth in the proportion of the young engaged in study, and the impact of the lower birth rate during the years of the Second World War, all this has given rise to an acute shortage of industrial workers.

Yet in the end, far more important than these explanations, for the failure of Soviet workers to produce as the system promises and needs, must be the attitude of the workers themselves, to their immediate employment and to the system which gives this employment its social meaning. According to Karol, indiscipline at work is officially estimated to cost the Soviet economy the loss of seventy-two million working days a year. The rate of absenteeism is not even evaluated in statistics, so as to avoid 'causing alarm'. And 'productivity in certain industries is so low that the workers seem to be practising the "go slow" technique'; as in the countryside the peasants seem to pursue 'a sort of passive resistance'.[10]

Evidence of such discontent and resistance is not, of course, evidence of incipient revolution. And it is not just that the repressive arm of the bureaucracy has proved itself long and strong enough to prevent or crush the emergence of any organized popular opposition. The ubiquitous interventions of the state, with the engrossment of all lawful organizational forms, seem to have succeeded in atomizing citizenship: isolating intellectual from worker and peasant; worker and peasant from one another; intellectual from intellectual, worker from worker, peasant from peasant. To be sure, in a totalitarian polity, especially one as vigilantly policed as is the Soviet, organized opposition must be secret; and to know, from outside, of efforts at organizing against the system, would be to know that these have failed. But the knowledge of such failure is also knowledge of the effort; and the apparent absence of failure at present, strongly suggests the absence of effort, from among the ranks of industrial labour or the peasantry. Attempts to circulate ideas of disaffection, as by the *samizdat* or clandestine publishing network, seem virtually confined to a few members of the intelligentsia. And the tight state monopoly of mass communications has so far ensured that such ideas should go unpublicized at home, or publicized only as the authorities see fit. By comparison, the control of information and opinion by the Tsarist regime was provocatively infirm.

Yet none of this can dismiss the challenge which must increasingly confront the Soviet system. If there seems to be no more as yet than reluctant collective acquiescence, with individual resistance revealed in the quality of labour given to the state, individual resistance can cumulatively assume a conscious collective shape, and reluctance effectively become in the process, revolt. The impact made on the economy by the continuing refractoriness of so many individual peasants and workers may itself promote an insurgent discontent with material conditions. Dissident intellectuals may still be shut off securely from the populace: but their very persecution may gradually dig an underground passage between. If the regime conceals its punishment of offenders, how is further offence to be intimidated from gathering force? Yet if the regime is to advertise the punishment, it must advertise the offence being punished: or the exercise rather loses its point.

Then, for all social categories, albeit in varying degree, time itself is undermining prevalent attitudes to what is possible and proper. The proportion of citizens who grew up in the dark years of Stalin's rule, not to mention those who can recall a pre-revolutionary Russia, must diminish; as the proportion with experience only of the post-Stalin bureaucracy must rise. The contrast of the past must yield less and less moral income.

And how may the regime insulate Soviet youth from the rebellious example of youth elsewhere? It cannot safely leave them to suppose that their counterparts under liberal capitalism may have more cause for contentment. Yet if it cites evidence of discontent by the young under liberal capitalism, not all the implications are safe. Not even the Soviet press is able, for instance, to report mass student demonstrations in the United States against the Vietnam War, without allowing that students in the United States demonstrate massively against the policies of their own government. And of course, as events in Eastern Europe have shown, student revolt is a phenomenon far from foreign to the Soviet empire. As the demands of sustaining the coherence of the system lead to less and less restricted travel within its compass, the phenomenon may well prove dangerously contagious.

But, above all, as with liberal capitalism, manifestations of challenge to the system only reveal that the challenge is essential: and so must develop as the system itself necessarily does. For the Soviet system, too, is based upon a moral commitment to the person – or what is Marxism at all positively about? – that its peculiar preoccupation with property represents itself as serving, but inevitably repudiates. And it is driven at once to explain and disguise the contradiction by what may be termed an inflationary materialism. Yes, runs the argument, the system may so far have failed to provide the values of individuality promised by Marxism. But this is an unavoidable prerequisite to producing the material abundance without which such values must be, as they are in bourgeois society, a delusion. And so, the less convincing the moral content of the system, the more important the prospect of material abundance must be made.

Yet not only does the prospect seem to recede as the Soviet

AN AGE OF REVOLUTIONS

system strains to approach it. By the very measure of material achievement which the system ultimately agrees with liberal capitalism in employing, it is bourgeois society, and not the Soviet interpretation of scientific socialism that is ahead; and, for as long as matters, looks likely to stay so. With all relevant riders of past and present imperial exploitation taken into account,* liberal capitalism does seem sheerly more efficient than the Soviet system in the provision – by quantity, quality, variety – of mere material goods. And sufficient citizens of the second know or suspect this, to make the first disturbingly more a source of yearning than of revulsion. The frontiers of the Soviet system are so ferociously guarded at least as much to keep its own citizens from leaving as to keep other citizens from entering undesirably.†

And why, indeed, should the system be preferred to the liberal capitalist alternative? Protestingly socialist, it rejects the despotism of the market and the dynamic of competitive consumption. Relatedly, it disparages and denies the conventional civil rights of the secure bourgeois order. And it invests its promise and its excuse in the moral incentives of collective service. Yet it subjects people at least as relentlessly to the property of the state as liberal capitalism subjects them to private property. Its bureaucratic despotism allows a personal freedom with still less meaning than lingers in the language of bourgeois civil rights. And its devotion to the moral incentives of collective service is displayed by discrepancies in material consumption so substantial and blatant as to need a Marx for their suitable indictment. The truth is that the system has long ceased to bear any but a deceitful resemblance to socialism: with the bureaucracy in place of the market as the groundwork of exclusive power; with collective service a synonym for the

---

*For, of course, imperial exploitation is by no means a liberal capitalist mono-poly. Even leaving aside the issue of internal imperialism, what but such exploita-tion was, for instance, the Soviet plundering of industrial installations in Manchuria before the Chinese revolution? And the system today does not sell its manufactures, including arms, to the poor world, and buy raw materials or agricultural produce, without in general extracting a profit from the transactions. If this profit is not always directly economic, but diplomatic or strategic, this is also true of liberal capitalism. Certainly credit expects a due return: and few loans by one or other state in the system do not carry interest charges.

†Article 64 of the Soviet criminal code makes any illegal attempt to leave the country a treasonable act: with a minimum sentence of ten years' imprisonment; and a maximum of death.

surrender of the individual; and with moral incentives finally reduced to the commandments of nationalism.

How long can such a system survive on a diet of its own deceits? With every moment that passes, its commitment to beat liberal capitalism at their material duel becomes less credible. Yet what is it to do? To ask that it abandon so morally mutilating a duel altogether, and substitute the priorities of personality for those of property: to ask, in short, that it become in reality a socialist experiment, is to ask that it change its very nature. The bureaucracy would resist to the end the revolution in social relationships involved. It would be fighting for no less than its life. And other important social categories, themselves resentful at the prerogatives of the bureaucracy, would vigorously oppose a socialism incompatible with their own prerogatives as well. The alternative, to which they are increasingly attracted, is for the system to become far more like liberal capitalism, along the lines of the reforms proposed in the letter from the three Soviet intellectuals.

The bureaucracy must, by the dictates of its nature, resist too, the inevitable dilution of its dominance that this alternative entails. But if driven, by the mounting problems of its incompetence and the social pressures that result, to secure what it can of the system by change, it is far more likely to follow the relatively conservative prescriptions of liberal capitalism than the revolutionary ones of socialism. Indeed this explains much of the remarkable difference in response by the Soviet regime to the reform movement in Czechoslovakia and that simultaneously being conducted in Hungary. This is not, certainly, to suggest that the Czechoslovak movement of 1968 was a clear or consistent socialist one. An important impulse was the yearning within the managerial and intellectual elites for just such changes in economic organization and civil government as the three Soviet dissidents listed in their letter. But the course of the movement; with the gathering popular experience of political expression, and in particular the searching idealism of the youth, at least raised the sufficient risk of a revolutionary socialist engagement that might engulf the country and endanger the whole Soviet system. The local bureaucracy was losing control of events, and the imperial centre had to re-establish the old certainties.

The Czechoslovak upheaval may have been set off by the issue of economic reform. But it spread so fast and so far because the moral fault on which the social order rested had accumulated such stress: from the discontent of the Slovaks* with their relative situation in the state, to the gathering popular resentment at the repressiveness of the regime. Beset by the failures of the economy under rigorous centralized bureaucratic direction, the central committee of the communist party had in October 1964 laid down principles of cautious economic liberalization which gave rather more responsibility to the professional managers. Prices were to reflect costs more closely; industrial development was to be financed largely from bank credits and the profits of industry itself; enterprises which showed a consistent loss were to be liquidated. But the experiment raised expectations without satisfying them. The party leadership had no intention of encouraging independent initiatives. Existing enterprises, grouped together in almost one hundred monopolies, operated bureaucratically, as the rest of society did. Prices rose faster than wages; and wages, faster than production. The individual monopolies hoarded their accumulated investment funds. The economic reformers, led by Professor Ota Sik, demanded further measures; and their demands revealed, as they promoted, mounting political dissatisfaction. In February 1967 the central committee agreed to consider the whole social role of the party, and in October adopted a report recommending that no one should hold office simultaneously in party and state. This was plainly aimed at Antonin Novotny, president of Czechoslovakia and first secretary of the party, whose conservatism had succeeded in uniting the economic reformers, the representatives of Slovak discontent, and the intellectuals against him. The party presidium, the pre-eminent repository of power in the Soviet system, itself proposed his dismissal as first secretary; and in January 1968 the 144-member central committee voted to appoint Alexander Dubcek, as a compromise figure against whom there was no significant body of antagonism, in his place.

It was the breaking of the gates. The central committee began debating issues with unprecedented frankness and vigour. It elected a new presidium, which accepted rather than dictated

*Some four million of the country's fourteen million inhabitants.

committee policies. Functionaries up and down the country, stunned by the sudden irruption of events, waited to see what the party's new leadership would do. And the party's new leadership, seeking mass support to withstand any conservative counter-attack, and bewildered by its very achievement of power, was carried along by, even as it conducted, the assault on the past.

The Youth Union asserted its right to be an independent organization, free to dissociate itself from party policies. An article in the trade union paper insisted on an end to party interference with the trade unions. The Scientific Council of Charles University in Prague declared that justified criticism by students should not be met by 'bureaucratic disciplinary action and repression'; and the Writers' Union demanded the complete rehabilitation of all those unlawfully punished before. The government dismissed the effective head of the state security services. Increasingly party leaders presented themselves on radio and television to explain their policies, answer questions, consider criticism. In the presence of first secretary Brezhnev of the Soviet Union, Dubcek addressed a meeting at Prague Castle to celebrate the twentieth anniversary of the communist party takeover in Czechoslovakia; and to an explosion of applause he announced that the party's policy was now one of elevating the 'struggle against' into a 'struggle for'.

Conservative bureaucrats were losing their posts – by the middle of April, only two of the ten regional first secretaries of the party under the previous regime were still in office – but for pensions, not punishment. And conservative spokesmen were free to argue against the reforms, within the party and outside. In a general excitement at democratic discovery, there was awareness enough of the threat that the old guard represented, but no disposition to intimidate or silence opponents as the old guard itself had done.

The new leadership presented its first policy statement to the central committee at the beginning of April. This conceded, to Slovak pressures, federalizing reforms; rehabilitation of those who had fallen victim to Stalinist trials; an end to censorship; and certain changes in the electoral law. Novotny was forced to resign as president of Czechoslovakia; and Dubcek's nominee, General Svoboda, who had supported the communist party takeover in 1948 but then fallen so far from official favour that he was free of the disrepute attaching to the exalted of the intervening years, was elected by the National Assembly in his place.

But the mood in the universities and the factories and the streets was beyond being satisfied by this. Workers who had regarded, as well they might, the call for liberalizing economic reforms with some distrust, were now excited by what seemed a searching social adventure. And the party itself reflected this new mood. District conferences refused to follow platform advice, and brought up new issues while discussing the old. Again and again party delegates objected to the official list of candidates for one or other commission. There were demands for further changes in the electoral law, to make balloting at all levels actually secret, and to ensure that candidates were selected by the number of votes they received rather than by their relative place on an official list. There was agitation to rid the central committee of its recalcitrant conservatives; and since only a full party congress could properly do this, the leadership was at last impelled, by the gathering strength of radical opinion in the ranks, to announce the holding of a congress in September.

More and more, what had begun as a movement of measured reform was taking on the prospect of a revolution: though of a revolution predominantly inside the communist party, and directed at realizing many of its own, for so long evaded or denied, ideals. As Professor Goldstucker, president of the Writers' Union, declared : 'We have no precedent for this. No communist society has attempted to democratize itself in this fashion. But there is no reason why we cannot evolve a new system of democratic socialism combining greater personal freedom with Marxism-Leninism.'

In the event, the reason was to lie outside Czechoslovakia, in the mounting alarm with which such an experiment was being viewed by other regimes within the Soviet system. Poland – where student demonstrations had been rigorously suppressed in March, and where disobedient intellectuals were under bitter attack – East Germany, Bulgaria, and the Soviet Union itself were deeply distrustful and hostile. Hungary, disturbed that its own economic reforms might be politically misinterpreted, issued dark warnings against 'anti-socialist forces'. Only Romania,

101

anxious for its maverick foreign policy, supported the right of the Czechoslovaks to pursue their particular development of socialism; while making it abundantly plain that no democratic stirrings would be permitted among its own citizens.

The crucial opposition was, of course, that of the Soviet Union. But to what was its regime so opposed? Total submission to the dictates of Soviet foreign policy was not the categorical imperative that it had once been. The Sino-Soviet dispute and the movement towards greater independence of Moscow among leading communist parties under liberal capitalism contributed to the need for more strenuous Soviet patience now. Romania had publicly and safely opposed Soviet attempts at having China condemned for heresy by an international conference of communist parties, with a disloyalty that seemed rather more challenging than anything that Czechoslovakia looked likely to undertake in international affairs. For all the Czechoslovak talk of improving relations with Western states in the cause of economic development – and how different was the view of Czechoslovakia in this, from that of Romania, or of Hungary? – there was clearly no serious support for any step so gratuitously provocative as the severance of the military connection with the Soviet Union. Indeed, the new leadership persistently proclaimed the inviolability of the Soviet alliance.

And if Czechoslovak economic discontent required some Soviet response, the provision of investment capital would surely have cost the system less overall than the military alternative. Certainly there was no reason to suppose that any liberalizing economic reforms in Czechoslovakia would by themselves have more impact on the character of property relations, at home or elsewhere in the Soviet system, than those already being pursued in Hungary. What evidence was there that the Czechoslovak workers and students and party radicals sought the handing over of their economy to private ownership? The evidence was far more of some integrated economic and political exploration for the personal liberty and equality which socialism was supposed to be about.

That, indeed, was the trouble. There was far too much concern in Czechoslovakia with making socialism democratic. It threatened the whole nature of government in the Soviet system. If the Czechoslovaks succeeded in developing social institutions, not least within the framework of the communist party, that served instead of subjugating the individual, what impact would this have on bureaucratic rule from East Berlin to Moscow itself? That communists should openly argue with each other about basic social policies, and proceed to engage the general citizenry in the argument, provided an example that citizens of the Soviet Union, not to mention other countries in the system, might feel themselves encouraged to follow. How, for instance, might citizens of certain Soviet Socialist Republics react to the success of Slovak agitation for some real measure of local self-government?

The Dubcek regime, responding to the expressions of external hostility, and itself concerned at the momentum of internal desire for change, warned against 'certain extreme trends and deviations', and 'local attempts to give vent to non-socialist methods'. But how far could or would the Dubcek regime command events? In April the central committee of the Soviet communist party demanded a relentless 'struggle against bourgeois ideology'. In May, *Pravda* attacked the 'anti-communist hysteria in Prague'. Dubcek himself visited Moscow and returned to report the anxiety there that democratization in Czechoslovakia might be abused 'to the detriment of socialism'. General Yepishev, responsible for political direction in the Soviet armed forces, declared that the Soviet army was prepared to do its duty if the 'faithful communists' in Czechoslovakia appealed for help.

In June Professor Sik, now a deputy premier, proposed a form of worker democracy: with workers' councils given powers of control over important management decisions, including those involving new investment, the distribution of profits and the planning of production. And near the end of the same month, the 'manifesto of two thousand words', with many distinguished scientists and the Rector of Charles University among the seventy signatories, was published. Warning of the conservative counter-assault, it advocated 'public criticism, demonstrations, resolutions, strikes and boycotts to bring down people who have misused power and caused public harm'.[11] The manifesto was rejected by the Czechoslovak presidium; but the Soviet press pounced upon it nonetheless, as representing the menace of 'counter-revolutionary forces'.

In the middle of July – a week after the regional meetings in Czechoslovakia held to elect delegates for the September congress of the party – party leaders from the Soviet Union, Poland, Hungary, Bulgaria and East Germany, gathered in Warsaw. They dispatched a joint letter to the Czechoslovak central committee, stating that the situation in Czechoslovakia was 'absolutely unacceptable'. The Czechoslovak reply, issued by the presidium and overwhelmingly approved by the central committee, rejected such foreign interference. *Pravda* then reasserted the terms of the Warsaw letter and, ominously, attacked 'right-wing anti-socialist forces, encouraged and supported by imperialist reaction'. At last, on 3 August, despite their reiterated unwillingness to enter into any but bilateral exchanges with representatives of other countries in the system, the party leaders from Czechoslovakia met their counterparts from the Soviet Union, Poland, Hungary, Bulgaria, and East Germany, at Bratislava. And on the following day a joint declaration, which implied certain Czechoslovak assurances, pledged 'all-round co-operation ... on the basis of the principles of equality, respect for sovereignty and national independence, territorial inviolability, mutual fraternal aid and solidarity'. Czechoslovak premier Cernik proclaimed at a mass meeting in Prague the country's allegiance to the Warsaw Pact and Comecon: 'we cannot be neutral'.

Then, on 10 August, the presidium of the Czechoslovak communist party published its long awaited draft reforms in the party structure. Those of a minority opinion, though required to remain loyal, were all the same to be guaranteed the right to go on disagreeing; and not only at meetings of the party but in the press. To make more difficult any one group's self-entrenching domination of the party apparatus, there was to be a choice of candidates for every post, with all elections by secret ballot, and a limit of twelve years' service for a member of the central committee or presidium. There were to be separate Czech and Slovak parties, with a federal Czechoslovak party above them and arrangements for the just representation of each people in the various bodies of this.

Such was far from all for which party radicals were pressing; but these seemed content now to wait on the September congress, and on the new central committee to be elected by it, for further reforms. Two days later, on 12 August, *Pravda* resumed its attacks. And on 20 August, the central committee of the Soviet communist party met in emergency session. The following day, troops from the Soviet Union, Poland, Hungary, Bulgaria and East Germany crossed the frontiers of Czechoslovakia. They found few in Czechoslovakia who regarded them as saviours. For saviours from what might they be? Civilian resistance was improvized, and, for all its apparent hopelessness, massive. Radio and television and press services reported from concealment the course of events, in a guerrilla war of news, until discovered and stopped. Ordinary citizens, unorganized, removed signposts, street names, house numbers, to confuse the invaders; drove cars and trucks across the route of tanks. Crowds demonstrated in defiance of bans and curfews, jeering at the invaders or gathering round to ask them again and again, 'Why?' That the invaders themselves so rarely lost their nerve and fired into demonstrations was significantly due to the discipline which the demonstrators themselves displayed.

Such spontaneous self-organization, evident also in sudden industrial strikes, announced the difficulties that a crudely imposed puppet regime would be likely to face. And the invaders moved with caution: working as far as possible through representatives of the existing party leadership, and only gradually displacing them. It was not long before a sullen popular submission was achieved.

But neither Czechoslovakia nor the rest of the Soviet system would ever be the same again. In the suppression of a social experiment being conducted by professing communists, to mass enthusiasm, towards a socialism that meant what it said; an experiment barely begun so that failure could not yet convincingly be claimed: the imperial bureaucracy betrayed its essential fear of what socialism meant; of popular processes; of people themselves. It was a confession of weakness that in itself could not but further undermine the moral supports of the system. And, above all, the promise of the experiment remained: its appeal enhanced by the very character of the hostility that it had excited.

Yet all the while, Hungary has been permitted to pursue reform which, under the sway of a still unchallenged bureaucracy, has brought it perilously close to the liberal capitalist pattern.

Material appetites are being sharpened by a market that admits of fewer and fewer restraints. There are scarcely more brands of Scotch whisky available in London than in Budapest, where cinemas carry colourful advertising to promote a particular choice. Inside the state-owned Luxus department store are Italian shirts for sale at 850 forints each:* or well above an average fortnight's wage for unskilled labour. A few steps away is the Ekszer jewellery shop, state-owned too, with a profusion of gold bracelets on display, priced from 9,000 to 12,000 forints apiece; and a Patek Philippe man's wristwatch offered for 24,500. Nearby, a carpet or a fur coat may be bought for 35,000 forints : or well above what a skilled industrial worker usually earns in a year. At the coffee shop of a local hotel, middle-aged women delightedly admire one another's rings. And at the Clara Rotschild shop of *haute couture*, the manageress explains the high prices. 'Of course here, it is not for the people. We have many foreign clients, mainly from Austria. And some Hungarians, yes. They buy here for special occasions, for embassy receptions.'

Such luxuries are ample evidence of those who see no need to conceal their material advantages. Apart from the top bureaucrats, who in the main continue circumspect about display, there are the more prosperous in the still relatively small but thriving private sector of the economy; managers of state-owned enterprises, and less elevated executives who supplement their salaries with income from secondary jobs in academic teaching or research; academics who supplement their salaries with income from secondary jobs in industry or government; technicians who have developed profitable productive processes. There are those lucratively situated in the professions, especially doctors with the appropriate private practice; and successful writers, musicians, painters and other artists, who are even permitted to spend abroad, on otherwise unavailable commodities, part of their foreign earnings. There are families where neither husband nor wife is in such highly paid employment, but where their

---

*or some £12 ($ 28.80) at the tourist exchange rate of 70 forints to the pound, which for obvious reasons favours sterling. All such figures apply to early 1970, when the author was visiting Hungary.

combined earnings reach the necessary level : as there are families, indeed, already to be included through the earnings of the husband alone, where the wife also is at work and bringing home a considerable income.

It is a category important enough for the present and growing number of those who belong to it. But, as its equivalent in liberal capitalist countries, it is much more important for the disproportionate social influence that it exercises: not least through the leadership in consumption that it gives. And of corresponding importance, too, for the impact of contrast, are those at the other end of the economic scale. An occasional beggar may be found outside the Luxus department store. Or, to quote one of Hungary's leading Marxist ideologues, 'there are, sorry to say, signs even of misery with us: among the old, on small pensions; among those with large families.' And in between, across the broad mass of social experience, are the myriad differences of means, that are more and more making of material consumption the basis of individual identity.

Indeed, this consumption exerts in Hungary a psychical influence of particular force. For it represents both the progress and the perimeter of social reform since the deeps of Stalinism; the period of closely controlled relaxation that followed, to be all at once swept away by the uprising of 1956; and the speedy Soviet military reconquest. Whatever the real character of that uprising,* there is now a general shrinking from any prospect of another. 'One 1956 is enough', comes the frequent comment. And for the time being, therefore, the rising standard of material consumption, so widespread if unequally shared, is enjoyed not only for itself, but as the very substance of social movement, in a politically paralysed environment. People stand and examine the shop windows in Budapest with an attention rather sharper than may be explained merely by the novelty of so much more to buy and so much more with which to buy it. Those displays of television sets and vacuum cleaners, cameras and cream cakes, foreign clothing and foreign liquor, are so many wall newspapers reporting the latest state of the nation.

*And the political disposition of many participants who subsequently settled in the West, combined with the not so remote fascist past of Hungary, may well suggest a more credible element of the merely retrogressive then, than in Czechoslovakia twelve years later.

As under liberal capitalism, such private consumption is essentially exclusive. It depends on discrepancies in the capacity to buy. And it therefore discriminates between one citizen and another by material worth. Furthermore, the material discrimination is inextricably a social one: a measure of social value. And this social discrimination is, in turn, inextricably a moral one: a measure of personal value by the society. To be sure, such is not explicit in Hungary's New Economic Mechanism. But it is implicit enough in the central message of the economic reforms: that the more a man contributes to the nation's material prosperity, the more he must materially receive, as inducement and recompense. Marxism revised has become 'to each, according to his ability'.

It is the market that must increasingly distinguish the contributions, as it increasingly distinguishes the rewards. The criterion must be material profit: for the individual enterprise; and within the enterprise, for the individual employee. The Danube Iron and Steel Works made a profit in 1969 of 1,200 million forints. Of this, the state took thirty per cent in taxes; the enterprise kept fifty-eight per cent for investment; and twelve per cent went in bonus payments to the employees. Such payments must reflect degrees of responsibility, and encourage competitiveness for promotion to higher reaches of reward. Thus, top managers might get up to eighty-five per cent of their annual salary in distributed profits; middle managers up to fifty per cent; and others up to fifteen per cent. In the end, it is the management itself that decides. At the Danube Iron and Steel Works, the bonus differentials were set at between thirty-four per cent and eleven per cent. Top managers received in all some 120,000 forints a year each; and the average worker some 30,000.* At a Budapest research institute for modernizing industry – a firm of management consultants – the most senior executive received, with bonus payments, 140,000 forints in 1969; the average worker, some 30,000; and the porter, at the bottom of the scale, 20,000.†

*Figures from a report in *The Times*, London, 30 November 1970.

†Figures from an interview with one of the management. These incomes may seem paltry, in exchange rate terms, by comparison with pay for similar employment in a liberal capitalist country. And to be sure, standards of material consumption are generally higher in such countries than in Hungary. But the exchange rate belittles the internal purchasing power of the

But competitive efficiency may exist as well between one group of employees and another on the same level in the same enterprise. In many of the major industrial concerns, the contribution of a particular work team to corporate profits will be rewarded by corresponding bonus payments to the technicians, supervisors, workers responsible: with each of these receiving his peculiar percentage, in keeping with his assessed share of the joint achievement.

The inegalitarian impact of all this is not denied, but defended, as necessary to the general good. 'If the manager of an enterprise making light bulbs is more important for economic progress than a blacksmith, the manager must get more.' The criterion is social utility. It is, if you like, inequality by function; rather than, as in the West, by ownership', argued an eminent economist. But is liberal capitalism itself not significantly shifting the source of social inequalities from ownership to function? Its tax system more and more discriminates against 'unearned', in favour of 'earned' income. The major corporations, that dominate the economy, are effectively less and less subject to control by a diffused proprietorship : while the managers and technicians on whom their prosperity depends, exercise commensurate power for commensurate rewards. And does not liberal capitalism claim, too, with scarcely less, or scarcely more reason, social utility as the excuse for its differentials? Would it not be possible, indeed, virtually to eliminate the private ownership of the productive means in Britain or the Netherlands, while continuing to promote a social system of rampant material inequalities?

Ah, but here it will all come right in the end, is the Hungarian reply. The present inequalities are merely a means for producing the material abundance that will in turn eliminate the inequalities, since everyone will then be able to have what he needs. 'In the spirit of Marxism', a professor of philosophy in Budapest explained, 'you must interpret the concept of equality according to historical processes. And you must ask not only how something is divided, but what it is that is being divided. We

forint; many prices, like those of certain basic foods, and most rents, are still fixed at a relatively low level; personal income tax scarcely exists, taking only a small slice of high earnings; and pension deductions, varying in accordance with income, do not exceed some seven per cent.

need to invest five times as much human labour in making a television set here as it takes in the United States. A low level of production allows only an equality in asceticism, as with the Chinese. At our present stage of industrial development, distribution can only be directed by achievement. What matters is that the socialist base of our society, in public ownership of the productive means, has been secured.'

Such ideological rationalizations are not convincing. If at the present stage of industrial development, society cannot produce sufficient quantities of a required commodity for ubiquitous purchase, why should the distribution be qualified by some assessed achievement of certain citizens, instead of being random? If only fifty thousand television sets, for instance, can be manufactured in any one year, without neglecting socially determined priorities, why should not lots be drawn for the fifty thousand families willing to purchase them? And if society puts a higher priority on television sets than on other commodities in production, why should the requisite shifts in the supply of labour and resources not be managed by the proper democratic processes of citizen equality?

To provide for superior and inferior claims to the possession of commodities, as relatedly for superior and inferior forms of employment, is to provide for a superior and inferior citizenship. It is incompatible with the morality of socialism, whose basis must be the equal if different needs of personality, and the equal if different social need of the individual job. If social efficiency can only be promoted by the competitive material incentives of unequal pay and unequal consumption, for what becomes thus an unequal personal value, then socialism itself must be seen as socially inefficient. But what is socialism about if not true social efficiency: in the full because free utilization of the productive possibilities within each person; in the creative relationship between the equal citizen and his community, that should serve as the ultimate incentive and reward?

Certainly, to suppose that socialism can be advanced by the temporary pursuit of private advantage, is perilous illusion. For how is the pursuit of private advantage, once established in social command, to be displaced? What reason is there for believing that a social system of economic inequalities will spontaneously abandon, rather than seek insatiably to promote them? Lenin, for one, saw none. And abundance itself is, surely, at least as much a social attitude as a material fact. By comparison with the living standards of most men, the United States has already reached a level of material abundance which should allow, on the Hungarian argument, an equality of consumption to all its citizens. But who would sensibly maintain that were a still liberal capitalist United States to be twice, or twenty times, corporately richer than it is, it would distribute its material product any less unequally? It would continue to promote poverty so that the rich might retain their meaning. And why, given twice, or twenty times, the present material product, should the cause of private advantage cease suddenly to be spoken or heard in Hungary? If every citizen has a motor car, there will be some whose distinctive achievements demand a special model, or a platinum wrist watch.

And indeed, how secure is the boasted socialist base of a society over which the exclusive material incentive holds sway? Marxism itself discriminates between the base, or economic foundations, of a society; and the superstructure, or character of authority, custom and prevalent ideas. Marxists have in general concentrated on the responsibility of the base for the superstructure: so that the character of bourgeois society, from the slum and the strip-tease show to the manipulations of the press and the deceits of the electoral process, comes essentially from the private ownership of the productive means. What the Maoist critique contends is that a change of the social base does not in itself transform the superstructure accordingly; but that, instead, the superstructure untransformed may proceed to change back the base. And the Maoist indictment is precisely that in abolishing private ownership of the productive means, the Soviet system did not create a classless society, but maintained an ultimately capitalist superstructure, which has inevitably begun to affect the base.

'Soviet experience shows that power, privilege and access to education can form the basis of class distinctions passed on from parents to children. Moreover, in trying to break out of the excessive rigidity of centralized planning, the Soviets and People's Democracies are resorting to economic incentives and market relations which, in the Chinese view, are inimical to

111

building a superstructure of human relations in a genuinely socialist form. There is, certainly, an important difference between using profits as a criterion of success in an enterprise and relying on profits as a motive for activity; but the Chinese maintain that the first will inevitably lead to the second.'[12]

The very concept of profit is a capitalist one. In a socialist society, goods should be produced and distributed as an integrated process in which every citizen shares. The consumer should be as much part of the light-bulb industry as anyone directly employed in it. The separation of industries from each other should itself have a solely mechanical purpose. The society – not the state, as an impersonal entity; but the people, as individual citizens exploring, discussing, discovering together – produces and consumes. Where in it is the room for profit? For at whose cost would the profit be made? And how should there be profit without cost to someone else? Once grant the criterion of profit, for the individual work team or enterprise, or for the state and its officials, and the society of unequal citizenship, of exclusive power and its corresponding denials, follows of course.

In a crucial rejection of the very socialism that they still profess, the Hungarian ideologues of the New Economic Mechanism claim that the state is, after all, only accommodating itself to the yet unready condition of human nature. 'We tried once', the explanation came from several, in much the same words, 'immediately after the war, to rely on moral incentives. It didn't work.' But how should it have worked, under a bureaucratic despotism imposing its social design in a travesty of its democratic pretensions? What moral incentive was admitted, but service to a state whose own officials apparently needed the incentive of exclusive power and its associated economic prerogatives? The social imagination of Hungarians did not fail; it was never given the chance to try. If human nature seemed capable only of pacing backwards and forwards across a small stretch of floor, this was because the social order had confined it in a cell. And now the reliance on the profit motive, on the private material incentive, is a last confession, of what was from the beginning a fundamental contempt for human possibilities. It is, all too pertinently, the same contempt which informs liberal capitalism: that the mind of man is, above all, moved by competitive vanity; by the greed for possessions and for power over others.

And now, indeed, when and how in its progress is the profit motive to be arrested? By the considerations of crude material growth to which the system is committed, such reforms as Hungary's New Economic Mechanism are clearly succeeding. Their success can only excite mounting pressure to follow their example in the countries left behind.*

And in the countries themselves ahead, it must excite mounting pressure for yet further example. Social categories which have climbed so high the slopes of private consumption, will want to climb higher; while those below are drawn on by the tracks of those above. And all the while, the claims of the material competition with liberal capitalism, will lend the force of an increasingly spurious ideological issue to the call of developed appetite. Hungarian management, encouraged by the contacts with Western business that the profits from foreign trade encourage, has begun to reach for the new prospects opened by the enjoyment of the already old.

Nor is it likely, on a Marxist or any other rational analysis of history, that social categories of growing economic privilege will fail to insist upon a corresponding political place. As the letter from the three Soviet intellectuals bears witness, the appeal of liberal capitalist economic reform is essentially associated with the appeal of liberal capitalist civil rights. And regimes like the Hungarian which yield the first, at least in part to escape the second, must sooner or later yield the second, as a consequence of the first.

Of course, the bureaucracy will not disappear from the Soviet system; any more than its liberal capitalist counterpart will cease for the while to thrive. Rather, it is here, in the relationship between state power and the private material incentive, that the two systems are being led, each by its own problems, to converge. Both are systems ultimately committed to

*In Poland particularly, since the recent turbulence that followed clumsy bureaucratic attempts at rescue from economic difficulties, the achievements of the Hungarian regime in material growth, and not least in narrowing the eyes of labour to the glitter of the market place, must exert a powerful appeal.

the moral thesis of property. Both systems must increasingly be confronted by the claims of personality. Both are likely to reach a common totalitarianism that promotes, as it seeks to prevent and to crush, the revolt of the individual.

It is out of this moral conflict, between property and personality, that the synthesis which is socialism must come: the society in which material production is the servant, not the master, of the individual; in which the collective imagination of the community is the source of authority; in which power is not exercised over people, by proprietorship or by office, but in which people exercise power by becoming themselves.

It is a conflict of which the revolutionary is the central, tragic figure. For he is victor and victim alike. He must be driven into acts that violate the very idealism that moves him. His commitment to personality is nothing, if it does not involve the infinite value of every person. Yet the system he assails is sustained by this person and that, who must challenge his life with their own. If he refuses the challenge, what has the system to fear from him? If he accepts it, how is he to avoid making himself like those he confronts? There is no answer: only the tormented moral occasion of his own mind.

He, least of all men, may conceal, in mere phrases, the impact of his meaning. To say that the system, in the very attainment of its repressive climax, must fall; that the advanced industrial state must become, the more intricate its functioning, the more vulnerable to attack; that the gap between order and chaos in such a society grows ever more narrow and easy for the resolute revolutionary to close: what measure of human suffering lies in this? Yet what measure is there now, when so many people spend all their lives in the cellar of their natures, shut away from their own possibilities? Justifications are the lids of moral sight. There is only the struggle of man for himself.

It is a struggle that must not wait. For how should history be left any longer to have its way? The past threatens the future as never before. The present nature of the material engagement is so wasting and poisoning the resources of man as to make revolution more and more the prerequisite of survival.

114

To see the interests of people as intrinsically exclusive; to see in the individual the substance for processing into profit; to see society as concerned supremely with control: such is to treat, as history has treated, man with a mixture of fear and contempt. The struggle against history, the struggle of the revolutionary, is the struggle to open a new moral dimension: the treatment of man with trust and with reverence. In the end what the revolutionary represents is the human promise alive in the very risk of love. To the fatal safe denials of the continuing past, he must be the reply.

PART II

THE DOORS OF PERCEPTION

'If the doors of perception were cleansed
everything would appear to man as it is, infinite.
For man has closed himself up till he sees
all thro' narrow chinks of his own cavern.'

William Blake, *The Marriage of Heaven and Hell*, c.1790

The dominant systems of government in the world today are based on a belief in man's ultimate social untrustworthiness. One moral root is in the very concept of original sin: in the Christianity of St Augustine who saw the nature of man in the greed and rage of the baby; in the Christianity of a Calvin who saw the salvation of the individual as impossible without the grace of God. Even when the revolt of Protestantism began invoking a certain democracy of the conscience in searching for the kingdom of heaven, it overwhelmingly rejected the social risks of encouraging a similar independence towards the kingdoms of this world. Luther himself consummated the attitude in a liberty of the spirit that yet accepted the subjection of the body to the secular sovereign. And if the progress of the Protestant revolt, with its constituent social impulse, demanded the right to overthrow one sort of secular sovereignty, this did mean forgoing secular sovereignty itself. Cromwell was no more accommodating to the free play of man's nature in social relationships than the king whom he had deposed.

The mainline of secular thought provided a similar service. Plato placed the rule of his ideal republic in the keeping of those fitted by nature and training to the task: since the mass of men were clearly unequal to it. Hobbes, in the wake of the English civil war, elevated secular sovereignty to its own heaven: since without it, every man's hand would be raised against his

117

neighbour, to make 'the life of man, solitary, poore, nasty, brutish and short'. Men covenanted together, for their own security, to obey a sovereign power; and this power had to be obeyed, except on the all but inconceivable occasion when it so denied its purposes that even the terrible state of nature promised an improvement.

This doctrine of social contract, variously amended, was morally central to the rise of capitalism, with the claims of property against the different prerogatives of feudalism. In perhaps its most celebrated variant, the American Declaration of Independence emphasized the duty of the sovereign to protect 'life, liberty, and the pursuit of happiness'; and the right of the people to alter or abolish it, 'whenever any form of government becomes destructive to these ends'. This new emphasis was, however, no less dependent on the old distinction, which it so influentially perpetuated: between people and sovereignty.

It is a distinction that prevails still in society. For where may the state and its institutions of government convincingly be seen to be the same as the people whose individual lives they direct? Where is social power not essentially exclusive? And the excuse remains the immemorial moral one. People simply dare not be trusted to be their own government. They must be protected from themselves, by processes in which they are necessarily involved but which exist outside of them. They must be ordered, for their own good.

There have been, too, the spokesmen of natural goodness, of a joyful impulse to create, that is turned to evil and destructiveness by the unnatural demands of the social order itself. But such – whether Blake or the early Wordsworth; Emerson or Thoreau; Tolstoy or Kropotkin – are considered merely as poets, possessed of a license to dream while others deal awake with the world. To the poet belongs the private life, where a man may explore the underground of unsatisfied desire, without endangering the delicate social balance. Public life is too important for visions.

This belief in man's social untrustworthiness has all too predictably been propagated by those who benefited from its acceptance. Those who have enjoyed sovereignty, together with those elevated by their patronage, have been quick to suppose and proclaim the horrors of anarchy, should the social order which they represented be disturbed. And they have done what

118

they could, as occasion required, to produce evidence for their predictions. What course the French Revolution would have followed, for instance, without the violent response of traditional power inside and outside France, cannot reasonably be established: but that this response was a significant factor in provoking the panic of the Terror, which itself nourished the rise of Bonapartism, is plain. When the social order of the market arrived to sovereignty, it supposed and proclaimed a similar choice only between its own dispositions and social chaos. And when it, too, in its turn, was assailed, as with the Russian Revolution, it sought to prove its point by its hostile military and economic pressures.

Its efforts were not without success. The tumultuous early years of the new Russia drained away from the revolution its socialist impulse of faith in the capacity of men, once released from the repressions of capital, to find their own way freely to the society of freedom. Trotsky's defeat was the defeat of socialist optimism, as Stalin's victory was the victory of the old doctrine, the old pessimism, in another form.* Far from withering away, the state under the Soviet regime flourished as never before, and the new social order regulated the lives of its subjects, in the name of their own greater good, with a ubiquitous precision unprecedented in history. The proclaimed dictatorship of the proletariat demanded popular submission, to counter not only the conspiracies of capital, but also the same enemy that was conjured up by capitalism: the terrifying unknown of society without some version of exclusive power. For the Soviet bureau-crat, as for the Western bourgeois, the distinction between people and sovereignty has been the prerequisite of civilized survival.

Inevitably, this distinction itself has produced resistance, and so evidence for its argument. The market has made poverty alongside riches; and crime in the making of both. Since money is the major measure of personal achievement, poverty is not

*Perhaps a perception of this sort lay within the more obvious meaning of what Trotsky declared to the Congress of Soviets, just after the October triumph: 'Either the Russian Revolution will create a revolutionary movement in Europe, or the European powers will destroy the Russian Revolution.'[1] And, of course, Trotsky himself, the creator of the Red Army, adjusted his optimism to events. Yet, by contrast with Stalin, he it was who represented the ideals of faith in revolutionary man.

only material want but personal failure, a rejection of claims to equal humanity by the social order. And as the character of much – indeed, a growing proportion – of crime in such societies suggests, this sense of personal failure takes its revenge in violence against property and people. Nor is crime restricted to the poor. For how can the law contain the appetite for money, where money means so much? Organized crime, considerable enough, constitutes only the tip of illegitimate profit. But to poor and rich alike, the power of money denies any identity beyond itself; and the search for some independent, personal meaning by the individual, explodes increasingly in crimes of hatred, guilt, despair, that are assertions of the self. Yet the response of the social order is not to question its essential purposes, but to fortify itself further. The laws and prisons multiply as witnesses to the peril which only the system prevents.

Similarly, under the proclaimed dictatorship of the proletariat, office in party and state carries prerogatives that produce a sense of corresponding deprivation among the many possessed only of citizenship. The deprived resist in a multitude of ways, from chronic drunkenness to formal protest. And the system claims the crime that it defines and excites, as evidence of the need for its continuing protective role.

Both systems are based on the evidence of a human nature which they themselves, by their very functioning, must distort. How may men be shown to be creative rather than destructive, compassionate rather than callous, generous rather than greedy, when the basis of their social order lies precisely in treating them otherwise? Those conscripted for warfare do not sign up as ready killers. Anyone who has had or watched bayonet practice, for instance, knows that men must be trained, even by brutalizing themselves with their own screams, to the readiness for killing. Whatever contributes to concealing or denying personality helps. In battle they shoot not at other people, but at other uniforms; or in a particular direction. Distance makes it easier. From a plane, a man bombs not children, but cities; not cities, even, but marks on a map.

The individual bourgeois or bureaucrat himself is not indiffer-

ent to the personal suffering of the individual he recognizes. It
is all too probable that either would be profoundly moved by the
sight of a person in distress. Yet both can – must, if they are
effectually to function – take with composure decisions that
profoundly distress other people.

> 'Between the idea
> And the reality
> Between the motion
> And the act
> Falls the shadow.'[2]

His system is essentially organized to prevent the bourgeois or
the bureaucrat psychically from seeing the person whom his
functions affect, as it prevents him psychically from seeing
himself as a person in the performance of his functions. Between
the actor and the act, as between the act and its impact, falls the
safety curtain of abstraction. Men become workers, and workers,
labour; men become managers, and managers, management;
men become investors, and investors, investment: as men become
officials, and officials, office; men become party members, and
party members, the party: while everywhere men become the
nation, and the nation becomes the state. Outside of what is left
to them as their private lives, their relationships are not personal.
They are those of implements in processes of power which deal
equally in abstractions: in supply and demand; profit and loss;
riches and poverty; order and anarchy; the progressive and the
reactionary forces of history; and everywhere, the people, the
nation, the state, the enemy.

The psychical safety curtain of abstraction that separates the
person from the processes of power, separates power itself from
responsibility. As in battle men merely follow orders, explicit
through the formal chain of command, or implicit in the
requirements of survival and victory: so under the systems of
bourgeois and bureaucrat, responsibility belongs always beyond
the commission of the act.*

The management of an enterprise under liberal capitalism
will, for instance, reduce its labour force – on such corporate

---

*The very language of social policy is more and more informed by war. There
are wars against crime and corruption, wars against ignorance and disease, wars
against want.

criteria as the state of the market, the availability of credit, the pressure of costs – without those who do the managing regarding themselves as responsible for the impact on those losing their jobs. No more will shareholders, most of whom may well never learn of the reduction in the labour force, regard themselves as responsible; even though this reduction belongs to their essential insistence that the enterprise should, above all else, make an adequate material profit. It is a moral dislocation that easily reaches extremes. What man would not feel responsible if by an act, in which he was a personal collaborator, another man was crippled or killed? What shareholder feels responsible if the enterprise in which he is invested, manufactures and markets products to cripple or kill other people?

Similarly, under the Soviet system, who feels responsible for the impact of official decisions and acts? To the measure that responsibility may in general be recognized as attaching to anyone, it attaches to those at the peak of the bureaucratic pyramid: the few who command the presidium, which commands the central committee, which commands the party, which commands the state. But these few are so psychically isolated, by the multitude of intermediaries and the whole complex corporate processes, from the person whose life their directives so intimately affect, that they would consider, if they considered at all, the acceptance of responsibility as impossible. And, indeed, were they to accept such responsibility, they could not be what they are, performing the functions that they do.

In the end, for the bourgeois and for the bureaucrat, as for the societies that they dominate, responsibility attaches only to the system itself. But the nature of both systems is to sustain a contradiction between morality and life. Each projects a distinct moral purpose – the bourgeois, that of individual freedom; the bureaucratic, that of social equality – and a common one, in the ascendancy of people over things. But individual freedom is incompatible with the prerogatives of wealth; and social equality, with the prerogatives of office: as the ascendancy of people over things is incompatible with the priorities of property, whether private or state.

With all responsibility, all real moral reasoning disappears down the division between what each system promises and how each system necessarily performs. Jehovah, when questioned, answered, 'I am what I am.' So, each system ultimately declares itself: with the excuse, 'because, of course, man is what he is.' And all those who serve the system derive from this their guilty innocence: their excuse for the depersonalization of people, with its betrayal of themselves; their self-promoting pessimism over the nature of mankind.

Alongside the established belief that men are morally incapable of being their own government must be placed the proposition that they have scarcely been given the chance to show themselves otherwise. At times, to be sure, they have reacted to the withdrawal of traditional order quite differently from the vain, fearful creatures, pursuing their own advantage at each other's expense, who have had to be restrained for their own sake. Ardent displays of collective vision and energy, of creative social commitment and happiness, have accompanied revolution. But this experience has quickly died. Has it done so for want of natural nourishment? or has it always been killed by the foreign forces and psychical fifth column of the old pessimism?

The answer lies in the development of an external sovereignty, an exclusive power, by the revolutionary process itself. Why do revolutions take place; and why, no less crucially, do they seem soon afterwards to stop and go into reverse? First, the record suggests, revolutions are not made by majorities but by minorities: elements peculiarly empowered, by the relatively large numbers they can mobilize in the principal cities, by their leadership of labour in dominant sectors of the economy, or by the armed force of which they can dispose, to defeat the traditional regime and change not merely the personnel but the character of rule. The mass of the population are generally passive; discontented with the traditional regime, even receiving insurgents in refuge, but not prepared themselves to join in actual assault. And the regime itself is so enfeebled, by a confusion of purpose, an incompetence of personnel, a sapping of support from sufficient social sources of allegiance, and a failure to solve the apparently paramount problems confronting the society,* that it not so much yields as collapses at last to its antagonists.

*These, of course, represent the clash between the old and the new moralities, but do not contain them. Thus the rise of capitalism against feudal privilege involved religious dissension in Stuart England; and the issues of representative

123

Then, with the traditional regime displaced, there follows a disappearance of mass inertia in a sudden sense of possibilities, a search for social designs to promote the now insurgent personality. Yet those who have led the revolutionary movement have formulated social designs in the process: designs demarcated by reaction to the character of the traditional regime and by the course of the struggle against it. The outbreak of popular enthusiasm accompanying the success of the revolution threatens these designs; and the need of its own social order to prevent the alternative of anarchy is propagated by the new regime with no less passion that it was by the old. Like a dying man circumscribing the conduct of his heir, the dying society qualifies its successor.

Now, from Maoism, has come the doctrine of the need for permanent revolution:* to resist or uproot the development of a self-promoting bureaucracy, which perverts the purpose of popular struggle. And whatever the failures or mistakes of its immediate application, this is a doctrine which does not close human experience yet again, as so many revolutions have done. It opens human experience, to the true meaning of man's equality.

This equality is not, of course, sameness. Indeed, it is precisely the engagement of society to particular forms of inequality that produces human sameness: whether in riches or in poverty, in cleverness or stupidity, in authority or subjection. It is these inequalities which inform the distinction between

government in colonial America and Bourbon France. The Russian revolution was importantly advanced by the haemorrhage of a war which the court had declared and conducted for what seemed to be its own purposes; as was the Chinese, by the inability of the Kuomintang to prevent or defeat the conquests and exactions by foreign power.

*The Maoist doctrine, which may be termed one of time, is not the same as Trotsky's earlier doctrine of permanent revolution, which may be termed, rather, one of space. For Trotsky, in accordance with Marx, revolution, to fulfil itself, and even to survive, could not stop at national frontiers, any more than it could stop at its 'anti-feudal' or 'bourgeois' phase. The final outcome could only be defeat or a united socialist world. It was against this that Stalin mounted his campaign for 'socialism in one country'.

For an analysis of the dispute and the course of its resolution in the Soviet Union, see Isaac Deutscher, *Stalin*, Penguin Books, London, 1966, pp. 284–95.

people and sovereignty; which are the psychical abstractions of the bourgeois and the bureaucratic systems. These inequalities are the uniforms which hide and deny the individual underneath. They are the means by which the person is himself made merely into a means.

To assert the equality of man is to assert his very individuality: against all attempts by society to make him no more than some constituent in a corporate abstraction. The equality of man is, in fine, the ultimate revolutionary doctrine. It properly demands a constant criticism of social functioning, a constant reassessment of social purpose, a constant readjustment of relationships between man and mankind. The doctrine of permanent revolution is, in consequence, new only in having become, with Maoism, so massively explicit. It has always been implicit in the doctrine of human equality.*

What is necessary is for the need of permanent revolution to be so widely accepted, for permanent revolution to be so influential a principle of human conduct, that no revolutionaries would, or safely could, attempt to make final their particular social design. Each revolution must be seen as no more than an experiment, from which men must move on, to experiment again and again, for the integration of their lives with their ideals. It is revolution because no aspect of society should be beyond the reach of experiment; no institution, no relationship so fixed, that it may not be displaced. It is permanent because one experiment must merge into another, for a continuous process of probing deeper; developing the social imagination further; cutting yet one more ledge from which human experience can climb to the next.

Is this a prescription for anarchy? But why should it be so? If one impulse of man is to be free, another is to be secure. Indeed, the tension between freedom and security will always exist, to inform the tension between the individual and society. It is the proper nourishment of the social imagination; the proper material of permanent revolution. It does not preclude, but presupposes some system of government, to represent the

*Whether Maoism intends what is implicit in its own doctrine: or whether, like the doctrines of equality in the French and American revolutions, it will become the occasion and disguise for a new external sovereignty, is beside the point. Such doctrines have a habit of outliving distortion by their own exponents.

claims that men must have on one another, if freedom itself is to be secured, and from security, advanced.

There are young revolutionaries in the United States and Western Europe today who have rejected the social commitments of liberal capitalism, but who do not reject social commitment itself. They constitute their own enclaves, each with its own system of effort and decision, and with disciplines none the less effectual – surely, all the more so – for being more spontaneous, experimental, personal, than the disciplines of the encircling society. They seem to have attained, some of them at least, in their tiny communes, a creative relationship between freedom and security, through the social cohesion of love and confidence; in place of the repressive conflict, the self-defeating cohesion of fear and distrust, that informs the culture they have renounced.

If anarchy remains a danger to be recognized and shunned, it is scarcely the danger in residence. And to be dismayed by the possibilities of anarchy in permanent revolution, now when the experience of man is so manifestly one of increasing authoritarianism, reflects a rather strange scale of social priorities.

Yet how is the person to cope with the experience of constant experiment; with the prospect, when not the existence, of profound social change? He is expected, of course, to cope, across the world today, with the assaults of property and office; with social systems increasingly bent on investing only the impersonal with value and purpose. And if he acquiesces in these assaults, it is because he is persuaded that such social experiences are unavoidable and, accordingly, normal. For example: man in the United States accepts, with apparent equanimity, as normal, that many of his number should be maimed or killed every year by the motor car; while deeply disturbed by the fewer of his number simultaneously being maimed or killed by a war abroad that he regards as abnormal.

Why, then, should permanent revolution, once it comes to be regarded as normal, be a social experience with which the person cannot cope? Indeed, a social experience with which the person can cope is the essence of permanent revolution. For, one may reasonably argue, coping is just what the person at present does not do. He subsists, stunted and guilty: knowing his abilities to be misdirected or wasted; his very meaning, denied: resenting the society responsible, and his own acquiescence. Truly to cope, by successfully confronting the challenge of his individuality, he requires the permanent revolution that encourages him to keep, and not the self-perpetuating order that compels him to break, his personal promise.

Is this all, however, not merely a euphemism for permanent violence, with men at one another's throat, to ensure each the ascendancy of his own system? We live so much with violence that the concept of a society without it, and pre-eminently that of a society engaged in revolution without it, seems an obvious nonsense. But is this not the trap of the old pessimism; the self-sustaining presumption of permanent betrayal? An essential objective of developing the social imagination, of promoting constant social experiment is, precisely, the ousting of violence as far as possible from human behaviour. It must be so: for violence is, surely, far more a symptom of diseased human relationships than a disease of humanity itself. And are these diseased human relationships to be regarded as inevitable? So was the plague long regarded.

Is violence the cry of the socially deprived? It must be possible to produce a society none of whose members need feel that he lacks so that another might have. Is violence greed? It must be possible for a society so to provide its members with a sense of their inclusive involvement in what they together make and enjoy, that such greed is in general seen as self-defeating. Is violence fear? It must be possible for a society in its functioning so to secure the equal rights of its members that fear ceases to be a social motive of any account. Is violence ignorance and hatred? But what should the development of the social imagination be about, if not that men should thereby employ their equal rights in meeting and searching each others' abilities and needs, so as to reach a sympathetic understanding? Is violence frustration? But what is the commitment to social experiment about, if not that men should employ their equal rights to promote in their relations with each other a process of personal achievement? Is violence despair? But what is permanent revolution about, if not to provide the individual with hope?

It does not follow that mankind will ever entirely rid itself of even what it may make into obvious nonsense; will ever entirely rid itself of violence. To believe in the infinite moral possibilities of man is to believe, as well, in the individual's possibilities for capriciously pursuing his personal defeat. But to believe in man is to believe this an aberration. And mankind can at least rid itself of those social systems that essentially make such aberrations into the norm; that essentially demand such personal defeats.

Social experience today, with its decisive denial of equal human rights, through the exercise of exclusive power; with its subjugation of people to things; with its irreconcilable conflict between the individual and society, morality and life: must be violent. For it must deprive. Greed and fear, ignorance and hatred are the preconditions of its survival. And its consequences are inescapable frustration and hopelessness. It is itself the violence of repressed personality. And the violence of repression excites, of course, the violence of resistance. Paradoxically, it is the very absence of permanent revolution that makes revolutionary violence so certain.

But does all this not entail a repudiation of the past, as though history had no content and no course; as though the present was not the cumulative product of reason? Is permanent revolution, indeed, not an infinitely dangerous – and inevitably futile – attempt to find the millennium by a leaping from the light of reason and the past alike? Yet why should this be so? The assertion of human equality, and of the related need for permanent revolution, must emerge from the very existence of the past. It would repudiate the whole meaning of man to repudiate history. The Chinese Red Guards who defaced the achievements of feudal art were ultimately defacing themselves.

It would repudiate the whole meaning of man as well, however, to be contained by the past. History must be a door opening outwards, not inwards. To be sure, the search to produce a social organization informed by human equality is a struggle against history. For history has taken shape from a contrary commitment. But to struggle against history is not to repudiate it. Such a struggle presupposes an acceptance of history, indeed, for all it has been, and all it has failed to be. And what is true of history, is true relatedly of reason. Of course, the present is the cumulative product of man's reasoning.

But it has been a reasoning too frequently dependent on the wrong assumptions; too frequently directed to the wrong objectives. Reasoning is a means, not an end. And those who have judged otherwise have over and over again served helplessly the most reprehensible ends. The Second World War, with its Belsen and its Hiroshima, abundantly attests to this. To reason within the moral confines of the past is to condemn man merely to repeat his mistakes, till in the stride of his technology he makes one mistake too many and disappears from time altogether.

How rational in fact is the present product of so much reasoning? Is it rational that some men should choke their lives with the commodities of a competitive vanity, while the lives of others are blasted by need? There was an ominous outcry once at the reported purchase of a diamond necklace by the Queen of France. Yet someone may securely buy at public auction today a single diamond: with a market equivalent, in material resources, sufficient to feed, clothe and shelter for a year ten thousand Indians, beyond the limit of their hopes. And how many in the countries of the rich do not act with a disproportion different only in degree? Is it rational that some men should set out scrupulously to determine what others read and hear and see and say and believe? How far have we reached since the grasp of the Spanish Inquisition? Is it rational that an advanced industrial culture should steadily be poisoning the very earth? What animal fouls its own nest?

Is it rational that governments should impose themselves, by varying degrees of violence, on people, and then demand as of right a sacrosanct sovereignty? Is it rational that mankind should allow any government to treat its own citizens as it pleases?* Is it, above all, rational that mankind should be cut up into arbitrary pieces, by frontiers and flags, armed forces and gross national products?

Certainly, to escape from the moral confinement of the past and its peculiar reasoning, requires a rejection of exclusive power as represented not only in, but by the nation state. For certainly,

---

*In the aftermath of the Nigerian civil war, to cite a recent instance, the provision of food to the starving was qualified by fear of affronting, let alone infringing, the sovereignty of a self-appointed military regime. And this sovereignty was regarded, by the spokesmen of modern civilization, as not only a political, but a moral argument against interference.

too, it is nationalism which has marked the decline of so many revolutions into mockeries of themselves, and which marks the entrapment still of so many professing revolutionaries inside history. Indistinguishably, the concern with national prerogatives, and the concern with prerogatives inside the nation, nourish each other. The regime of unequal property has been fostered by, as it has fostered, nationalism in the United States ever since the assertions of human equality in the American War of Independence. The Soviet bureaucracy has fostered, as it has been fostered by, Soviet nationalism, ever since service to party and state started consuming the commitment of the October revolution to man.

And indeed, it is becoming increasingly clear, there can be no cure for the infection of humanity by contending nationalisms, in treatment that intrinsically invigorates the virus of nationalism itself. The development of an international rather than a supranational authority, for instance, has inevitably secured and advanced national preoccupations: making the United Nations an instrument for simultaneously accommodating and encouraging the exclusive demands of national interest. And meanwhile, the conflicts of nationalism refractorily fester: to deflect the resources, the ingenuity and aspirations of men, from pursuing the indivisible enrichment, moral and material, of their lives, to the destructive sustenance of corporate competitiveness.

Significantly, the separatist cohesion of tribalism or of racialism has fallen into common disrepute, while nationalism itself commonly commands respect and even reverence. For, to the degree that any but an inclusive human cohesion may be regarded as rational at all, tribalism and racialism are at least as much so as is nationalism. The tribe is rooted in relatively close blood relationships and in a peculiar integrity of political and economic organization, language, religion, morality and art. The race encompasses distinct physical characteristics, for perhaps the ultimate in separatist simplification beyond the difference of sex. But the nation is often no more than a flurry of the past, frozen in movement: the manifestation of a conquest, or of a struggle against conquest; of a shift in the course and material of trade; of a grasped sectional ascendancy. It may cut a tribe in two; or enclose tribes with nothing but an immemorial antagonism in common. It may contain members of two different races, with those of the one practising a corporate discrimination against those of the other; or different peoples of peculiar culture, language, religion and social attitudes, with an aggrieved sense of their inadequately served separate identities. It may exclude a people whose culture, language, religion and social attitudes are the same as those of its own; who have far more that argues for their common, than that argues for their separate citizenship. What rational purpose informs the division of the Ewe into nationals of Ghana and of Togo; or the integrity of Nigeria? the common citizenship of Malaysians; or of Canadians? the separate existence of Argentina and Uruguay? And what rational purpose may be found to inform the respective nationalisms of the United States and the Soviet Union: the very reasoning behind whose revolutionary origins denied the exclusive commitment that nationalism represents?

To be sure, nationalism has contributed to liberating man from certain forms of subjugation: but it has done so only in the process to substitute others. Indeed, its subjugations are those which its apologists all too readily denounce in tribalism and racialism. And this all too ready denunciation betrays an awareness of how arbitrary, how irrational is the nature of the nationalist engagement. It is Caliban seeing himself in the glass, and asserting his claim to be Prospero by concentrating concern on the repulsiveness of the reflection.

Yet if nationalism ought to be discarded, as perpetuating and promoting the depersonalizing separatisms of the past: ought not, too, by the same argument, the conventional engagement to class struggle? To suggest this is to raise the swarms of ideological platitudes. But the challenge presented by the development of such engagement so far, has to be met. Of course the struggle against liberal capitalism must not be abandoned. It must and will exist for as long as there are some men who privately own and control the means of production; and, in consequence, others correspondingly deprived. But it must be a struggle not of abstractions, for exclusive objectives: in which, whoever the victor, the person is victim. A struggle of classes, as the past has abundantly demonstrated, is, like the struggle of nations, in the end a struggle against personality itself. The victory of labour becomes the depersonalizations of the bureaucratic society, as the victory of capital is the depresonalizations of the bourgeois. The struggle against capitalism must be a struggle by the person, for the person; not by labour, for labour; if it is to be a struggle by and for humanity.

Nor, it becomes ever more evident, is the struggle against the private ownership and control of the productive means the only, or even the overriding, one. The struggle against capitalism must exist, too, where the means of production have been wrested into state ownership and control: and where people are made to serve state property and institutions, in the class interests of those who command the state, or are paid for their collaboration by the superior enjoyment of services and resources. It is a struggle that must continue until the means of production belong equally to all people: until property and institutions exist only to serve the individual. It is a class struggle because it is a struggle against the very existence of class.

Is this a repudiation of Marxism? But to repudiate Marxism would be as destructive, and absurd, as to repudiate history. Rather, like history, it must be used to open, not to close. Marxism perceived a crucial aspect of human experience in time, and a crucial aspect of timeless human experience. Mankind is alive, if ill, but not living in Victorian England. History did not come to an end there and then; nor even later, in the Soviet Union, with Lenin. There has been not only the substantial change in the processes of capitalism, but the course of several revolutions in the cause of socialism, to consider. We have seen how such revolution has, in its bureaucratic development, travestied its own avowed moral purposes. And we face new problems, and new possibilities, in an advanced industrial technology that would have seemed like idle dreaming a few decades ago; that was, in fact, long dismissed in professingly socialist states as an anti-Marxist invasion of mankind's preserves.* But, above all, the Marxism that was a striving for the classless society: that saw economic equality as fundamental to human equality, and human equality as fundamental to the proper value, the very individuality of individual man: this will be valid for as far as the future stretches, no less than it was valid in the past.

*The Soviet rulers, for instance, anathematized the computer: until its exploitation in the United States seemed to promise such material success, that their dogmas had to find room for it.

All revolutions that fall away from a total human commitment thereby betray the humanity that gave them meaning,
and hang themselves in their own despair. All revolutionaries
who fail this total human commitment thereby become reaction-
aries: seeking not to liberate, but to subjugate; substituting the
dictatorship of prerogative for the democracy of personality;
and being consumed, inescapably, in the process themselves, as
people of individual promise and need, by their particular
separatisms. Their failure is finally a failure of faith in the
social imagination of man. They carefully contain it, for fear of
where it may lead them; and being contained, it wastes away.

We are not confined, as other ages have been, by natural
scarcity. The scarcity that exists, we contrive ourselves, or
ourselves allow. Technology and psychical incitement can always
extend the demand beyond the supply. If every family has a
motor car, or two motor cars, or three, competitive consumption
can be concentrated on the illusive or real superior functioning
or appearance of one make over another; or on the private
ownership of a rare computerized kitchen. And scarcity can be
maintained by assiduous neglect: by permitting the self-advance-
ment of the difference between knowledge and ignorance,
assertiveness and submissiveness, the riches and poverty of
material equipment.

Scarcity, indeed, remains a basic premise of social organization
both in the countries of liberal capitalism and in the professingly
socialist states of the Soviet system still today. To liberal capitalism, the factor of scarcity is proclaimed as permanent: to be
kept, however artificially, in crucial play. Whatever the growth
in productive capacity, there must be goods sufficiently scarce to
confer a corresponding distinction on those who have them: to
characterize, and accordingly excite, personal achievement; to
sustain the dynamic of competitiveness. But in the Soviet system,
too, scarcity is an increasingly artificial factor. Substantial discrepancies in the private ownership and enjoyment of goods
continue to exist, and are even, where measures of greater
market emphasis have been introduced, widening: excused as
constituting the temporary material incentives for economic

growth, towards the equality in abundance that will one day be communism.

Create wealth, cries liberal capitalism, by the disciplined drives of unequal consumption, and all citizens will consume more and more. Create wealth, cries the Soviet system, by the disciplined drives of unequal consumption, and there will in time be enough for all to consume equally. The disciplines are different – if diminishingly so – as is the avowed objective. But the effect of both engagements is the same: they promote, as they employ, the factor of scarcity.

All this begs, of course, the vital question of what material wealth is. Both systems simply assume that material wealth is what they are busy producing. But let us take two societies, A and B, with a population of twenty million in each. The first, with a gross national product valued at fifty billion dollars, has three million colour television sets; seven million private motor cars of various makes; and the latest models in intercontinental ballistic missiles. But it also has three million citizens living in slums; more barbiturates swallowed per head of population than books read; and an urban air so thick with industrial waste that people wear masks to breathe through when walking in the streets. The second society has no colour television sets; it has no private motor cars, but a public transport system rapid, frequent, and in easy reach of everyone; it has no missiles. It has no slums, since its citizens are housed with an equal decency that encourages opportunities for individual taste; there is small call for sleeping pills, and a large appetite for books; while industrial waste is carefully controlled to keep the air clean. And its estimated gross national product is twenty billion dollars. Is B less than half as materially rich as A? Indeed, will the society of moral wealth, where men best develop their individual abilities in an inclusive cause, not produce as well the most material wealth, in an integrated process?

The common cause of both the liberal capitalist and the Soviet systems, that scarcity permits an equality only in denial, is a self-promoting association of moral and material delusion. Advanced industrialization already allows the means for satisfying all reasonable needs of physical nourishment and comfort. Societies with such equipment have now only to decide what not to produce, so that they may produce for different purposes. And the means would increase with the appropriate investment. It does not follow that everyone would live as do the rich today. That is just what would be materially impossible; even if it were not physically so. Indeed, it follows that for some, perhaps many, citizens, standards of consumption must fall. But they will fall so that standards of living for everyone may rise.

What enormous productive facilities would not be released, for instance, and what measure of environmental pollution removed, by switching the emphasis of transport from the private to the public forms? How much human talent and energy would not be released for far more productive endeavours, by applying the machine not to feeding the endless auction in consumer vanity, but in freeing people from trivial jobs? For millions of men and women to be employed in sweeping streets or collecting train tickets or wrapping sweets is absurdly prodigal of human resources. How many engineers and architects and chemists are there not among them, buried alive in the lack of opportunity? And this, to be sure, raises the ultimate issue. How much productive capacity would not be added by the elimination of poverty itself? Even before they reach school, numberless children have their minds stunted by their environment; their sense of limitation inculcated, in kitchen and alley, by the precedents and precepts of parentage and neighbourhood. What is not lost to society in the process? And how much more is not lost in attempting to protect riches against the reaction of want and resentment? As how much is not squandered, in machinery and technical skills, by military expenditure?*

Inevitably such societies of advanced industrialization will become more creative themselves only if they enjoy less than they can for the while, and give instead, to end the existence of riches and poverty in a communion of mankind. Societies that remain strongholds of prerogative against deprivation outside, will remain strongholds of prerogative against deprivation within. The ramparts of the state, and the ramparts of the social order inside it, are counterparts of each other. The costs

*In his book *The Science of War and Peace*, Robin Clarke[3] estimates that one-fifth of the world's scientific manpower and more than $200,000 million a year are consumed by the military. The last figure probably exceeds the entire material product of the poor countries, with some two-thirds of the world's population.

135

of a separatist commitment are indivisible: as are the gains of the commitment to humanity.

Apologists for the separatist commitment would doubtless deride all this as romanticism; claiming to be realists. But are they not propagating, rather, their own romanticism: parading in the nakedness of the past that they take, deceived and deceiving, for the clothes of the future?

It is as though all men had gathered round a single pool, to jostle, fight, kill one another for water: with some hurriedly filling pot after pot, in a clearing made and guarded by guns, to increase still further a store evaporating in the sun; while others lie beaten and dying of thirst; and in the tumult, more water is spilt than ever gets drunk. And below, in the earth, nearby is a river running ready, its hidden presence betrayed by increasing signs. But who will leave off the struggle at the single pool: to dig, and let the water up, to form another pool, and another? Why if the river is there, has its water not burst to the surface before? And if some men will move away, to dig, will they not die of thirst in the heat; while those they have left behind only drink the deeper? And so no one will go from the pool, though there is enough there for all to drink and dig together. And the river underground runs ready but undisturbed.

Of course, it will not be easy, it will need great courage, to abandon the factor of scarcity. It will be like that abandoning, five centuries ago, of the belief that the earth was flat: sustained by what we differently believe, but with the cry in our ears that we are bound to sail over the edge or be consumed by monsters. And, to be sure, we will achieve as little, perceptibly, at once, as those whose ships left the harbours of an old world so secure in its very fears. But humanity owes it to itself – for what else is it for? – to make the leap from the past into the promise of its own capabilities. What has primarily been a problem of consumption, with men scrambling for exclusive enjoyment of insufficient resources, is now primarily a problem of production, with the promise of plentiful resources for inclusive enjoyment. Given the right social investment, man will be able to choose what and how to produce in excess of all that traditional need demands. From being enclosed in a passivity of consumption – and what is, essentially, more passive than the rich and the poor, labouring in their separate ways merely to consume? – human experience will become active and open: integrating work and art in the exploration of personality. What variety will life then not offer? In place of frontiers and flags, ambassadors and armies, each man will be his own identity, his own anthem: in a patriotism and a poetry of mankind.

PART III

THE CREATIVE SOCIETY

'I must Create a System, or be enslav'd by
another Man's;
I will not Reason and Compare : my business
is to Create.'

William Blake, *Jerusalem*, 1804–20

The capacity of a human being to surmount the most formidable
personal handicaps, through the care and encouragement of
others, is surely beyond dispute. The instance of Helen Keller,
made blind and deaf by infant illness, and helped by the
imaginative endeavours of her teacher, to become a person of
imaginative endeavour in turn, is widely celebrated. And how
many other human beings, variously disabled, have not been led,
by the proper will developed through the help of understanding,
to lead unexpectedly productive lives?

It was not so long ago that addiction to hard drugs like heroin,
and even to alcohol, was supposed virtually incurable. Treatment through enforced abstinence scarcely ever escaped repeated
relapse. But Alcoholics Anonymous and in the United States the
Synanon communities for treating drug addicts have recorded
substantial success in curing the incurable: each, by infusing
determination into the addict himself, through the development
of new personal relationships.

In Alcoholics Anonymous, the addict is encouraged to
acknowledge his condition, to others and so to himself; to learn,
from the experience of others, that his condition is not hopeless;
and to find in other people a source of comfort and self-confid-
ence, from a sense of mutual belonging and concern. Synanon,
founded by a member of Alcoholics Anonymous, takes the
process further. The drug addicts live in communities of their

own until satisfied that they are permanently cured: helping each other by example and care. And they employ a peculiar symposium technique* by which, in groups of ten or twelve members, they expose and explore together their grievances, their anxieties, their aggressions, their longings, their past and present relationships: in an attempt to understand themselves and each other, and reach thereby a productive sense of their personal purpose. It is significant that, far from becoming dependent on an insulated self-indulgent community of withdrawal, such groups soon spontaneously extend their interests and activities into seminars on politics, history, art; in preparation for meeting the challenges, and helping to change the quality, of the social experience outside. Certainly a visitor to Synanon communities receives the impression of individual addicts, young and old, not only finding rescue from the drugs which have been filling so emptily their lives, but with wonder discovering capacities, in themselves and other people, to which they had clearly been blind before.

And significantly, too, this therapy of social drama, as a compassionate and creative force, is more and more being employed by men and women with problems far less acute, but in the long run no less corrosive perhaps, than drug addiction or alcoholism. In Britain and the United States, for instance, there are groups meeting in variations on the theme of the Synanon symposium. Some concentrate on movement rather than speech, in a social drama of dance; some use masks or blindfolds to begin overcoming their fear and distrust of other people. All, however differently, seek to surmount the sense of sterility, of loneliness and loss, in their separate lives: by reaching, in a new social communication, the new possibilities of themselves.

Should we not learn from the curing of illness, how to be well? And how should we start if not with the child in the school? Walter Bagehot, in Victorian times, perceived what is no less valid today, in the era of executive rule through president or party secretary. 'The best reason why Monarchy is a strong government is, that it is an intelligible government. The mass of mankind understand it, and they hardly anywhere in the world

*The word 'Synanon' is a portmanteau word, from 'symposium' and 'anonymous'.

understand any other. It is often said that men are ruled by their imaginations; but it would be truer to say that they are governed by the weakness of their imaginations.'[1] It is this weakness which it should be the paramount purpose of education to dispel.

Bertrand Russell, in his book on *Power*[2], suggests ways of seeking 'to produce independence of mind, somewhat sceptical and wholly scientific, and to preserve, as far as possible, the instinctive joy of life that is natural to healthy children'. He would have broadcast to schoolchildren contending eloquence on all aspects of all topical issues, so that teachers might subsequently excite examination of the arguments and 'insinuate the view that eloquence is inversely proportional to solid reason'. He would have the techniques of producing irrational belief, as in advertising and propaganda, counteracted as early as infant school, with children required to choose between two classes of sweets: 'one very nice, recommended by a coldly accurate statement as to its ingredients; the other very nasty, recommended by the utmost skill of the best advertisers.' He would have the teaching of history conducted in a similar spirit, with study of how illustrious orators and writers in the past defended such positions, as 'the reality of witchcraft' and 'the beneficence of slavery', which are now generally recognized as absurd. He would proceed to the closer past, by having newspapers compared with each other and then with official history at times of popular hysteria such as war. And he would have, positively, through such studies as music and poetry, science and history, the nourishment provided 'upon which the better emotions can grow'.

There is obvious sense in all this. Yet it misses the crux. Such would belong more to the equipment than to the direction of schooling in the creative society. Education should be informed by two major, interconnected purposes: a resolving of the conflict between freedom and security; and an integrating of morality and life. Thus, it would encourage an understanding that all power should be inclusive, belonging to all people equally and reflecting in its functioning their equal value. It should reveal how the individual and society are inseparable aspects of all human development, in a relationship which may be, must be one of tension, but which should use tension to discover and not

141

to deny; why every man should be personally concerned and personally responsible for the personal impact of all he does; that things should exist for the sake of people, and not people for the sake of things. In short, what the school should be concerned primarily to promote, according to the advance in ability from age group to age group, is experimental democracy: in a civics of the child, not the text book.

The achievement of drama is the internal enactment for the spectator of events on the stage. The power of the play is commensurate with the degree to which it is experienced, not merely observed.* Shakespeare's *Lear* is a supreme example: and is, indeed, at the centre of the issues still confronting society. The doctrines of Machiavelli profoundly stirred an English imagination emerging from a feudal morality. And one dramatist after the other dealt with the apparent contradiction between the requirements of worldly success, or the dictates of realism; and the injunctions of traditional virtue, with their worldly failure. What Shakespeare does in *Lear* is to convey this seeming reasonableness of evil: of rejecting kindness and love for self-interest; trust, for fear.

'Goneril: A hundred knights!
'Tis politic and safe to let him keep
At point a hundred knights; yes, that on every dream,
Each buzz, each fancy, each complaint, dislike,
He may enguard his dotage with their powers,
And hold our lives in mercy. . . .
Albany: Well, you may fear too far.
Goneril :   Safer than trust too far.'

Edmund, Goneril, Regan seem to have all the evidence of the real world on their side. Lear *is* capricious. And Goneril *is* wise to deny his capriciousness a dangerous equipment. Yet who, experiencing the play, does not reject the wisdom of the realists for the foolishness of the morally 'natural': of Kent, Cordelia, the Fool? What the Fool himself says, has the edge.

'That sir which serves and seeks for gain,
And follows but for form,

---

*As the relatively uninhibited response of the audience in children's theatre indicates.

Will pack when it begins to rain,
    And leave thee in the storm.
But I will tarry; the fool will stay,
    And let the wise man fly:
The knave turns fool that runs away:
    The fool no knave, perdy.'

The experimental democracy of the classroom must be internally enacted as it is externally displayed. Children should not merely be told to see for what these are, the quicksands of exclusive power; the corrupting cosiness of indifference; the self-defeats of competitive acquisitiveness. They should experience them, with a teacher who provides the draft but encourages the play as far as possible to write itself. To suppose that, within such a dramatic framework, facts and, much more important, the skills of learning and judgement, could not be acquired, is to assume some discrepancy between the development of individual intelligence and of social relationships. On the contrary: the two developments are inseparably essential to what should be the process of education.

Certainly, to suppose that all this would rapidly produce disintegration and chaos in the classroom is contradicted by the notable strides, in standards of intelligence and spontaneous discipline, made where primary schooling has experimented with the rudiments of such techniques. Children from slums in the East End of London, arriving at their shabby schools with a resistance to learning and discipline alike, have profoundly responded to the encouragement of their capacities for expressing themselves in art, in argument, in collective research. The children develop their own discipline, alongside their interests, their insights, their imaginative relationships with each other and with their teachers. How much more creatively, spontaneously disciplined would they become, in being prepared for a dynamic role in society at large. The bowed head over the fixed desk before authority at the blackboard is the proper training only for the politics of mass subjugation: of the distinction between sovereignty and people.

The effort at promoting social imagination should not, of

course, be limited to the schools. The objective must be for the civic drama of the classroom to meet and merge with the processes of social exploration outside. And this might best be achieved in the political neighbourhood: in the immediate social environment of the school, organized into a council of government.

The Neighbourhood Council*

There seems no reason, with the numbers involved in such a neighbourhood, why this council should not practise direct democracy, or the participation of all citizens directly in decisions. Such a council would control the functioning of the school. But it should also be able to decide, for instance, the particular character of a local library or arts centre; and even, if within manifest limits, the particular economic enterprises that the neighbourhood contained. The assembly of citizens should have the power as far as possible to choose its own way of life.

And between the democracy of the neighbourhood council and the democracy of learning within the school itself, should exist a productive play of tension. The teachers would be common to both experiences, as members of the school and the council. But the pupils as well should be free, indeed encouraged, to participate in the council's meetings and decisions. Children wishing to express their desires and ideas at an assembly of the neighbourhood would, surely, be worth having and hearing there: for what they were; and for what in the process they would become.

But direct democracy is not invulnerable to distempers of despotism. Numbers in themselves would not ensure compassion or wisdom; prevent prejudice or caprice: even given the preparations here proposed. Yet precautions that denied the principle of equal citizenship would sacrifice much more than they saved.

The Neighbourhood Tribunes

The jury system recognizes the ability of adults, chosen within

---

*What follows is a suggested system of government for the creative society. It comes from certain positive principles, which may at least open a positive argument about social change. Professing revolutionaries are commonly challenged for being only negative in their attitudes. It is a challenge that they should not shirk.

certain criteria, from the supposition of sanity to the payment of property taxes, but without any special training, to decide on so delicate and momentous a matter as the legal innocence or guilt of a human being. There are countries, too, notably in Scandinavia, which have developed the institution of the Ombudsman : an official selected to supervise the workings of government, and intervene against abuses of authority for the protection of individual liberty and rights.

The jury system has in the main proved remarkably resistant to the vagaries of public temperament. And it has proved in the main, too, more equitable, more generous than the solitary prerogatives of judges, with their customary prejudices : their deference either to the commitments of their class, as in Britain, or of their electoral, often party-machine engineered careers, as in the United States. Its weaknesses have been largely those of the law: the limitations of the letter; the priorities of property, reflected in the very membership of juries; the pressures to protect the social order, regardless of changing moral claims to the contrary. The Ombudsman has served to inhibit bureaucratic arrogance and secure at least some citizens, with the sense of initiative to complain, from the misdeeds of authority. But a single office, under single command, to supervise a society of several millions, must be remote from the concerns of ordinary experience, and run the risk of becoming like the bureaucracy it is meant to correct.

Every neighbourhood should have its own tribunes, to regulate the working of institutions, ensure the proprieties of power, and resolve any conflict of rights: in a borrowing of what is best in both the jury system and the role of the Ombudsman. Such tribunes might be twelve in number; should be selected by lot from within the neighbourhood; and should serve not for a single occasion of judgement, but a set term – perhaps six months – so as to procure the advantages of some continuity. With the number of citizens in a single neighbourhood kept to a few thousand, this procedure would soon enough include a significant proportion in tribune service; and the spread of such experience might well be further ensured by disqualifying from the draw all those who had previously held the office. Certainly a major source of democratic failure in advanced industrial society is the concentration of effective government in relatively fewer and fewer hands. The process must be reversed, with the exercise and experience of power diffused as far as possible; to produce the ultimate safeguard against abuse of authority, in the mass demystification of politics. The right to be chosen for tribune service should start no later than the age of sixteen: not only because youth is an organic part of society, with its own involvement in collective choice; but also because the political development of the individual, and so of the entire society, is enriched, the earlier that it is practically directed. But since this must be an arbitrary demarcation, each neighbourhood should be left to decide at what earlier age to set the start.

Every citizen should enjoy access of appeal to the tribunes, whose decisions would be supreme within the neighbourhood: subject, of course, to the limits laid down by the society at large. They themselves would, for their term of office, take no part in the council's operations: since they might be called upon to review these, and should never be judges in their own cause. Doubtless they would be reluctant to contradict the express will of their neighbours. But that they would be expected, nonetheless, to rely on their own judgement, even against the most strongly held majority opinion, would be essential to developing the dignity, and promoting the purpose, of their office. And since each citizen without previous service might find himself a tribune at the next selection, such independence from temporary popular pressures, would be in his own, as well as in the general, interest to establish.

That the tribunes might seek to abuse their authority for private ends, would be made unlikely by the shortness of their terms and by the size of the neighbourhood. Moreover, their own decisions could be reversed by succeeding tribunes; and would be subject, on due appeal, to the authority of the regional tribunes.

There is a case to be made for verdict both by simple majority and only by unanimity. The first procedure would be easier, speedier; and the second, safer. But, on the whole, verdict by nine out of twelve tribunes, or a majority of three to one, seems a circumspect compromise.

The Region
To pose the economic independence of the neighbourhood is to

declare its absurdity. The division of labour may well be the basis of capitalism, private or state; but it is also the basis of industrialization, and of any escape from the confinements of a subsistence culture. Yet joint undertakings should avoid just such social units as presently prevail. The city, the suburb, the small town, the rural community: these are entities whose intrinsic separateness from each other makes them corporately exclusive; and their respective inhabitants accordingly estranged. But then the nation state, for reasons already given, is no answer either.

The region of inter-neighbourhood collaboration should be one which includes industry and agriculture, shopping centres and countryside, in an organic union. And if such regions might have to differ at first substantially in area and population, the objective must be to make them gradually less and less unequal: so as to secure not only a balanced environment within each, but as far as possible a balanced environment for all. How many citizens such a region would most effectually encompass, it would be idle, without experience, to estimate. But it is only reasonable to suppose an order of several millions.

Regional Government
For populations of such size, direct democracy, as practised in the neighbourhood, would be impractical. Yet to depend on current forms of representative government would be to invite the politics of party machine and manipulated apathy. The logical progression of the neighbourhood system already outlined would suggest a regional assembly, to which each constituent neighbourhood would, by secret ballot, directly elect two representatives: from a list of twelve selected by lot. Again, the objective should be to diffuse political experience; and the term of office should not only be set at one year, but disqualify the holder from ever serving another such again. Since many hundreds of neighbourhoods would be involved, and continuity so frequently if necessarily interrupted, government would also have to contain an executive, or regional directorate, with a permanent civil service at its disposal.

The regional directorate itself should be a comparatively small second chamber, the executive section of a single parliament; and its members, one hundred and fifty in number, should not serve for a term of more than three years, or be permitted more than a single term. Every third year the duly elected regional assembly would in turn choose the regional directorate from a list of its own members: half by lot, and half by secret ballot. And the directorate itself would then elect a first secretary: to lead the government and take overall responsibility for its policies, including the appointment of secretaries and their assistants to take charge of the various administrative departments. Collectively, such government should not encompass a majority of members; but it would have to command one. And members not serving in the government would constitute an opposition of independents: from among whose number sufficient support would be necessary to sustain the government on issues of confidence, involving major aspects of policy. The defeat of a government on such a vote would automatically produce its resignation, and the election of a new first secretary, commanding majority support, to lead a new one. The chairman, who would preside over the meetings of the directorate and interpret the rules of its functioning, would himself be specifically elected by members of the assembly, from among their own number. A special vote of no confidence, supported by at least three-quarters of the directorate, could unseat him: but only for a successor to be duly elected by the assembly then in session.

The regional assembly would, of course, make the laws and control finance: considering and passing, rejecting or amending the annual budget presented to it by the regional directorate. And members of the government should, therefore, be able to speak, if not vote, at its sessions. Since for two out of every three years, however, the regional directorate would face an assembly which had not chosen it, clashes between the two houses might be expected not infrequently to arise. And since the whole emphasis of such a system would be on political experiment, and on the expansion of personal liberties, rather than on conformism and the restraints of precedent, this should be all to the good. But if government itself is to survive, possibilities must exist for resolving parliamentary stalemates.

In the scenario that follows, it must be supposed that the pressure for settlement would persistently increase; and that popular opinion within the neighbourhoods and the region at large would encourage the surrender of one or other house, if compromise proved impossible. But the eventuality of a popular opinion sufficiently divided and a collision of principle sufficiently momentous, must be confronted.

In the first instance, with one of its major policies rejected by the assembly, the government might choose to accept the verdict and amend its programme accordingly; or resign, leaving the directorate to constitute a new government, capable of commanding a majority and willing to pursue a policy acceptable to the assembly. If the directorate refused to countenance such a change, however, the two houses would meet and vote jointly, so as to provide an opportunity for collective consideration of the issue and prevent too small a majority in the assembly from prevailing. If the policy of the government were then still to be defeated, and the directorate remained insistent upon pursuing it, the issue should go to a referendum : the result of which would automatically dissolve, for due reconstitution, the defeated house. Meanwhile, of course, previously accepted administrative policies, with the budget to provide for them, would continue to operate.

At no stage of this political process, could the association of men to promote a particular policy be prevented – for what else is government or opposition about? – except in so far as it conflicted with the laws of society. But these laws should themselves prevent the development of permanent parties which sought to enjoy exclusive power and exercise corporate discipline over members of the various social authorities. The distinction would inevitably be one which the society interpreted from experience: in accordance with its changing objectives, and through the judgement of such supervisory representatives as the tribunes. Some legal provision, against conspiracy to deprive the citizen of his equal rights, would form the basis on which the issue would have continually to be joined. But certainly no citizen in social office, whether belonging to the government or not, should be permitted to retain membership of any political club or caucus: since such would restrict his necessary independence of judgement, and confront his functions with the claims of a separatist loyalty.

If the system here outlined provides for a regional executive that should convincingly be kept from developing an effectively authoritarian social role, the problem of a surreptitiously exercised irresponsible power, through the civil service, remains.

149

Interfering too drastically with the permanent basis of the civil service would probably do more harm than good. If it would be crucial to diffuse political experience and responsibility as far as possible, it would scarcely be practical to do the same with special skills. Town planners and electrical engineers perform functions essentially different from those of elected legislators and executives. Here the emphasis should be on safeguards against arbitrary appointment or dismissal. But between the regional directorate and the technical ranks would be those in the internal management of the civil service: the departmental administrators and their assistants. And it is here that the dangers of bureaucratic entrenchment would most manifestly exist. To begin with, the service of administrator or assistant in any one department should be limited to only two years, so as to prevent the development of private domains and promote experience of different problems and situations. It could not but be ultimately beneficial for administrators of the public works department to assume responsibility for education and take with them the knowledge of related needs and difficulties; for an assistant in a department such as that of justice, to have encountered the challenges of the education department.

Furthermore, to avoid the abuses which attend secrecy, all correspondence between the executive and the civil service should be open to public examination: with access enjoyed, on demand, by any citizen. And specific committees of the regional assembly, with half their membership chosen by lot and half by secret ballot, to supervise the work of the various departments, should be able to summon, in public session, the appropriate administrators, for inquiry into their policies and for recommendations to the regional directorate.

The Judiciary

The perfect society could dispense with judges, juries, lawyers and police: since, by definition, there would be no crime, and law itself would exactly correspond with the will and conduct of every citizen. Since the creative society would still be imperfect, however; since perfection would always be precluded, indeed, by the essential impulse perpetually to experiment and improve; an apparatus to interpret and enforce the law would be necessary. In the end, of course, the incidence of crime, and so the extent of the apparatus to deal with it, would depend on the character and direction of society itself: the degree to which the individual citizen believed that his purposes were being served by the whole complex of social institutions. Yet the apparatus of the law would itself be part of this complex, and would have, therefore, to be made compatible with the other processes of government. To deprofessionalize, to democratize politics without simultaneously deprofessionalizing, democratizing the interpretation and enforcement of the law, would be impossible.

It would only be consistent with the nature of the politics previously outlined if neighbourhood councils were themselves to be responsible for the local administration of justice. Each council would elect a judge, to serve an unrepeatable term of two years: and would provide from among its own citizens, for every trial, a jury chosen by lot. A separate official, the examining magistrate, elected by the council for an unrepeatable term of a single year, would decide, on the evidence provided by the regional office of prosecution and on the submissions produced by the regional office of defence, whether there was any case to answer and so any trial to be held. Verdicts on minor offences, such as involved punishment by small fines or a few days of imprisonment, would be subject to revision on appeal to the neighbourhood tribunes. More serious verdicts would automatically proceed to the regional appeal courts, which would review the conduct of the trial and the propriety of the sentence.

These appeal courts, whose number would be dictated by need, would each consist of three judges chosen, for an unrepeatable term of a single year, by lot from among former neighbourhood tribunes;* and a regional jury, chosen by lot from among all citizens, for an unrepeatable term of six months. Further regional courts, similarly constituted, would deal with regional offences, as where the injurer and injured came from different neighbourhoods, or where regional interests were involved; and special cases such as the interpretation of contracts. But in all instances, further appeal would be permitted, with

*Were the regional framework to be established simultaneously with the neighbourhood one, so that no such former tribunes yet existed, judges would at first be chosen by lot from among ordinary citizens of the region.

agreement from the regional office of defence, to the regional tribunes.

Harold Laski, in *A Grammar of Politics*,[3] proposed for criminal cases a public defence office, provided by the state, to ensure that no citizen, accused of a serious offence, would face trial without a proper defence. And, for civil cases, he suggested public offices attached to every court and appointed by the local authority: to provide advice and information; encourage private settlement through mediation; and prepare cases, with the appointment of defence counsel, for trial. There seems no sufficient reason, however, to divide the responsibility for public defence between local offices for civil cases and more centralized offices for criminal ones. Regional offices could well enough deal with all feasible demands, and themselves contain separate sections for civil and for criminal justice.

Whether each neighbourhood should have its own office of prosecution is another issue. On the whole, it seems best that both prosecution and defence should emanate from outside the area where the examining magistrate, the judge and the jury would all be selected. The regional offices would, of course, belong to the civil service, and be subject to the same conditions of performance as applied to other departments. What would be lost in local cohesion would here, surely, be more than compensated by the gain in impartiality and overall balance.

The Police

Similarly, the police should be recruited and organized on the basis of the region rather than that of the neighbourhood. But the police force constitutes a special case. For it is the police who represent not only the enforcement of justice and the protection of rights, but so easily also the opposites of these, in the enforcement of injustice and the protection of outrage. Indeed, by the nature of their function, the police promote authority rather than freedom; obedience rather than experiment; and constitute a constant temptation to the abuse of power by the government they serve. It is not enough to make a revolution. As the past has abundantly demonstrated, it is necessary to protect a revolution once made. And to protect a revolution without sacrificing many, if not all, of its principles in the process, has proved the most difficult endeavour of all.

It is all too probable that the police, for as long as society required to employ them, would present an authoritarian risk. But the risk could be significantly reduced by deprofessionalizing the police and diffusing the experience of their function. To be sure, society has seen nothing impractical in sending ordinary citizens to the battlefield, after a mere few weeks of training, when occasion called. And it is to be doubted whether service in the police is plainly more difficult and demanding than military service in times of war. Further, most countries still have compulsory training in the armed forces for all physically and mentally able citizens of a certain age. There is, therefore, nothing apparently impractical in a police force to which all capable citizens would be summoned, by lot, for nine months or a year of service. No one would have to serve more than one such term, and terms would so overlap as to ensure a majority of the adequately trained in the force. In a society with the essential emphasis on freedom and experiment, it would be useful for citizens to encounter, at some period in their lives, first-hand some of the accompanying problems; for however they might gradually diminish, problems there would be. And in a society the mass of whose citizens had served in the police force, to uphold a genuine democracy, it must be all the less likely that a conspiracy of authoritarian objectives would succeed. Certainly a government would find a police force of ordinary citizens less amenable to being employed in advancing or sustaining abuses of authority than a force of professional police accustomed to unquestioning obedience.

A permanent, civil service core in the force would be necessary, for the specialist functions that demand years of training and experience. And here, as with other specialist civil servants, the emphasis must be placed on protection against arbitrary appointment or dismissal. Permanent administrators there would have to be as well, subject to the same provisions against bureaucratic entrenchment and secret deliberation as applied to their counterparts elsewhere in the civil service. But the police, by reason of the potential threat that they must always pose, would require particular supervision by society. A regional commission of twelve, selected by lot from among former neighbourhood judges, for a term of a single year, would provide a public report on the operations of the police; and examine any relevant complaints, from inside or outside the force, for recommendations to the appropriate authority. Above all, any use of the police for activities likely to endanger life, as in the suppressing of civil disorder, would require the formal agreement of the commission by a vote of at least three-quarters, or nine of the twelve members.

The Treatment of Crime

Revenge, of course, should have no place in any humanist punishment. The payment for crime should be founded on three principles: compensation, where possible, for the injured; the protection of society against further injury; and the rehabilitation of the injurer. The first principle has ample and persuasive precedent in primitive society. A man convicted of having stolen from another should be made to return what he has stolen; or, if unable to return it, should be made to provide, by his labour if necessary, its material equivalent. For crimes against the person, to be sure, there is no equivalent recompense; but the payment of material damages might yet be of some service, if more for what the injurer would have to give than for what the injured would get.

The second principle is, or should be, dependent on the third. To isolate criminals from the rest of society without meanwhile integrating them in social allegiance and purposes, is to protect society for no longer than the terms of imposed isolation. Indeed, as the evidence of such isolation overwhelmingly suggests, society protects itself at the cost of endangering its members all the more afterwards. The prisons of advanced industrial countries are poor advertisements for their deterrent power. They are, on the other hand, excellent schools for the confirmation of conflict with society and for the professionalization of crime. Short of imprisoning every discovered offender for life, therefore, society cannot protect itself properly without eliminating from the mind of the offender the impetus to offence.

Such impetus, however, may well be the fault of the society. And whether crime is a symptom of personal or of social sickness will significantly depend upon its nature and incidence. Every year the regional assembly should be required to consider the crime rate, as it is required to consider the budget; and frame its findings, where advisable, in relevant legislation. Any increase in the overall rate for three successive years, would summon the additional scrutiny of the regional tribunes.

Meanwhile, treatment of the criminal might well demand his imprisonment, not only to protect society, but the more effectively to advance the processes of cure. Yet this should never imply circumstances of deliberate degradation. Prison conditions, of diet and accommodation and access to films or records or books, should not significantly differ from those prevalent outside. And if labour were imposed, for the payment of material damages, it should conform as far as possible to the ability and desire of the citizen imprisoned. Indeed, the genesis of the individual crime might largely lie in the incompatibility of the criminal's usual work with his ability and desire; and a crucial aspect of his rehabilitation, therefore, would be the discovery of his proper employment. But where no such incompatibility existed, it might often be found best to let the criminal continue in his former employment, among his free associates.

His labour, however, should never take so much time as to interfere with the related therapy. And this should be based on the techniques of social drama that have proved so productive in the treatment of alcoholics and drug addicts. The objective would be ultimately the same : that in communicating with each other, criminals would proceed to communicate with themselves and with society: would discover the source of their conflict, and thereby reach out to confront and resolve it. And as in the treatment of alcoholism and drug addiction, former alcoholics and drug addicts, the embodied experience of cure, have been essential to the success of such group therapy, so prison officials should as far as possible once have been prisoners themselves.

If the prison service is by definition a special case, that would need corresponding safeguards for its government, the democratic principle must in all social activity be maintained: or the effect of a prison sentence would be not to resolve, but yet further to increase the conflict between the prisoner and society. In control should be a prison commission with twelve members: of whom six would be selected by lot from among the members of the regional assembly; and six, also selected by lot, from among all the prisoners in the region: for an unrepeatable term of a single year. This would supervise the general functioning of the prisons;

would consider complaints and take appropriate action; and would confirm or reject recommendations from the various prison councils.

For each prison would have, in a counterpart to the neighbourhood council, an assembly of officials and prisoners to manage its affairs; and in particular to recommend the release of such prisoners as seemed to have been cured before the completion of their sentences. Certainly, to continue holding prisoners fully rehabilitated, would be to defeat the whole purpose of the service and risk reversing the rehabilitation itself. Any unfulfilled obligation to meet material damages might as well, and perhaps better, be undertaken in free employment. In short, prison sentences imposed by the courts should be regarded as the limit of punishment for offenders who proved themselves unresponsive to therapy. Indeed, it may be argued that no time limits should be imposed by the courts, since imprisonment would be primarily concerned with cure. But limitless sentences might encourage abuses of their intention. And the laying down of a limit, even without cure, would accordingly protect the liberty of the individual.

Mass Communications

Among the major issues of government must be the management of radio and television, the press and other publishing. And if private ownership and control must be discarded by the creative society, as providing some citizens with undue power, the record of state ownership and control has scarcely been one to excite confidence in the capacity of this alternative to promote the free flow of ideas.

Nor is the currently radical proposal for the control of communications by all those who work in them a socially equitable one. Why should editors and interviewers, cameramen and printers enjoy the prerogative of deciding what the mass of citizens should read and hear and see? To be sure, theirs might well be the initial direction of the forms to which their careers were devoted; theirs the initial responsibility for encouraging a creative communication between the producers and consumers of ideas, with the ultimate aim of eliminating the distinction between the two. But there must be instruments – other than the mere measurements of immediate audience or readership response – by which both the individual producer and the individual consumer would participate in the processes and influence the course of communications.

On the level of the neighbourhood, where communications should as far as possible have a local identity, and where at least radio and television might well offer feasible opportunities, the professional producers would be members of the citizen council. And any conflict between them and the bulk of the council would go to the neighbourhood tribunes for resolution. But no majority of professional producers, council and tribunes should be permitted totally to command communications. Every citizen in the neighbourhood should be entitled on demand to a certain amount of radio and television time a year: so that even if only a few minutes were the acceptable allotment, he could express his opinion on anything he chose: or, by combining with others, promote a minority view at commensurate length.

Furthermore, specific programmes, both regular and emergency ones on issues of flaring public concern, should invite direct viewer or listener participation. As the short period of experiment in Czechoslovakia revealed, citizens will readily respond to serious opportunities offered by mass communications. Radio and television especially became a stage for the creative consideration of social issues: with people exploring each other's ideas, by telephone from home to the studio, or before the cameras in the street. The medium is what authority makes of it. If popular participation in radio and television seems so often in advanced industrial society to consist of record requests or panel games, this is surely because nothing more has come to be encouraged, where it is even allowed.

Neighbourhood newspapers, if only weeklies or issued irregularly, should also not be beyond the resources of communities with a few thousand citizens each, and should be similarly organized to produce a dynamic relationship between professional producers and the public.

The region would, however, be the more practical entity for a daily press; for some book publishing; for a radio and television that could employ world-wide correspondence services or even afford the dispatch of their own correspondents, and that could commission original works of drama, music, and other art.

On this regional level, too, initial responsibility would rest with those themselves involved in producing the various services, whether as permanent or casual contributors. An annual meeting of all in a particular service would elect an administrative committee; and regular, perhaps monthly, meetings would help to ensure that administration did not stray too far from the mass of the producers. As elsewhere in society, the objective would be to spread the experience of responsibility; and no producer would be entitled to serve more than a single term on such an administrative committee. Furthermore, should the committee and the mass of producers find themselves at serious loggerheads, a special meeting, that recorded a two-thirds vote of no confidence, would be able to dismiss the serving committee and elect another, for a full year of office, in its place.

As with neighbourhood communications, regional services, from radio to the press, would provide significant time or space for citizens to consider social issues : with the participants selected by lot. And if the probable regional population would make it impractical to allow the individual citizen a specific allotment by right, a sufficient number of citizens – say, one thousand – would be entitled, on due demand, to employ so many inches of newspaper space, or so many minutes of radio or television time, for the advancement of a common opinion or cause.

The ultimate control of regional communications should, of course, be vested in the regional democracy. But this ought not to mean the regional directorate, which might then seek to employ such powers to the advantage of a particular government; nor a committee of the regional assembly, which might attempt to employ them against the regional directorate in a parliamentary clash. Since a neighbourhood basis would be no less necessary to a democracy of communications than to other aspects of democratic functioning, and since the independence of such services from political authority should be promoted, a special commission to control communications should be selected, by lot, from an annual list, to which each neighbourhood council would contribute six nominees.

This commission, with twenty-four members serving for an unrepeatable term of one year, would supervise the policies pursued by the administrative committees and general meetings of producers in each regional service: radio; television; the press, both newspaper and magazine; the publication of books. And it would have the right, by a two-thirds majority, to order changes in such policies.

Since too precise a command of the budget by the regional assembly might permit, and even provoke, disguised political interference, the assembly would vote only a total annual sum for all communications, which the commission would allocate to the different services. But security of employment for the producers themselves would demand an additional safeguard; and any dismissal would require a three-quarters majority vote of the commission.

The Arts

The encouragement and enjoyment of creative art would significantly depend on the opportunities provided by mass communications. But the importance of such art to the creative nature of society itself, its willingness and ability to experiment with its institutions, is so fundamental that the momentum of development would have to be secured by additional measures.

Each neighbourhood council should receive from regional resources an equal allotment, which the neighbourhood might then augment from its own, specifically for expenditure on the arts. And, indeed, it should be possible for every neighbourhood to have its own arts centre, with at least a local theatre and art gallery. But the neighbourhood would be inadequate for what the arts could produce only at the cost of large resources, and with the investment of a large public.

Each neighbourhood council would accordingly elect one representative, from a list of six chosen by lot, to serve, for an unrepeatable term of one year, on a regional arts council. This would have its own budget: with revenue supplied in part from payment for material used by the mass communications, and in part from a proportion – fixed only at its minimum – of regional assembly resources. It would elect, for a three year period, and from among its own members, an executive committee: with a relationship between the two, similar to that of assembly and directorate in the regional parliament.

Regional Tribunes

That clashes between different social authorities, over priorities

159

and even principle, would occur, is only to be expected. And that the individual citizen would always require protection from the abuse of public offices, however popular their basis, cannot reasonably be doubted. Regional tribunes, sixty in number and selected by lot, for an unrepeatable term of nine months, from among all citizens in the region, should accordingly enjoy power to act as guardians of personal liberty, and ensure the proper functioning of institutions.

They would be enabled to order the retrial of any criminal or civil case; to delay the application of any decision by any authority within the region, even one from the assembly or directorate, for three months, while the decision was duly reconsidered; and to resolve any conflict of rights between different authorities, except where otherwise specified.* Individual citizens might appeal to them directly for intervention. And if such appeals reached a number beyond their capacity to handle, they would select by lot those to consider.

If it is complained that such men would have no special training, the answer is that ordinary citizens would be precisely those required to perform such functions. For if ordinary citizens are incapable of protecting and promoting a democracy, then democracy itself is a dangerous delusion. And if it is supposed that such men, equipped with so much power, might themselves abuse their responsibilities, at commensurate social risk, it should be remembered that their departure from office after nine months of service would be automatic.

This does not mean, of course, that regional tribunes would be incapable of mistakes or impervious to gusts of public opinion. It is likely that service in such an office would itself produce the courage of independent judgement and the imaginative reach that it required. But safeguards there should be : if only to encourage the tribunes in the exercise of their own authority. No decision of theirs on any issue should be valid without a two-thirds vote in its favour; and no decision on a constitutional issue, concerned with clashes between institutions or with the propriety of policies pursued by duly chosen authorities, valid without a three-quarters majority. In turn, tribunes would be immune to arrest or prosecution of any kind not only during their term of office, but for a full year afterwards. This, it is to

*As in the clashes between assembly and directorate.

be hoped, would help to prevent any temporary popular antagonism, however widespread and heated, from seeking to intimidate the tribunes: though without, in the process, putting them for too long above the law. Furthermore, any decision duly taken by one set of tribunes would be reversible only by the due, three-quarters majority vote of their successors: or, on appeal, by the world tribunes.

Inter-Regional Collaboration

If the neighbourhood would be the basis of this system, and the region the natural extension of the neighbourhood, this is scarcely where social organization should end. Art and mass communications should as little be contained by regional frontiers as certain forms of economic enterprise. Yet where is inter-regional collaboration to begin and end? A professional opera company, with sufficient resources to commission new works for its repertoire, might require an audience and subsidy most convenient to two or three regions; a socially efficient land transport system might have to involve twenty or thirty; a suitable computer industry might need two or three times that number again. The point is that it would be impossible to know, except by the functioning of such collaboration itself. What is clear already is that any unit as fixed as the nation state is an arbitrary one: too large for some forms of regional collaboration; too small for others; and, even where feasibly of the appropriate size, not necessarily of the appropriate resources. A particular region might well need to collaborate with some regions for one purpose, and other regions for another. And, indeed, such separate collaborations should be encouraged, to prevent the development of inter-regional power blocs. The answer must lie in a loose arrangement which would vary with the individual project.

Secretaries of transport from the regional directorates involved in the construction and functioning of a transport system, would meet as members of the operating inter-regional delegacy: as would administrative commissioners for opera, in an inter-regional delegacy to supervise and promote the activities of any joint company. It is here, of course, that some assurance of continuity would become an important concern. If several regions decided, for instance, to collaborate in a vast waste-disposal programme, involving the investment of commensurately vast resources, a particular participating region should not be permitted simply to withdraw, at any stage, in response to a policy shift by its own directorate, regardless of the damage inflicted on its associates. Yet, if some law of contract were to operate in such undertakings, there would have to exist an authority to interpret and secure it. And it seems only proper that this authority should not itself be fixed, but vary, as would the participating regions, from project to project. For any one project, accordingly, an arbitration panel should be established, of representatives from all the regions concerned. Each relevant regional assembly would select by lot from among its members two, who would serve on the particular panel for three years, and then give place to a different two, similarly chosen. The primary objective of such a panel would be, of course, a settlement to which all the constituent regions subscribed. But if this were to prove impossible, a three-quarters majority of individual panel members would be sufficient to fix the terms of compensation for any breach of contract: and this would be binding, unless reversed on appeal to the world tribunes.

The World Parliament

Ultimately, however, inter-regional collaboration would best be promoted and secured, as would the whole political system of neighbourhoods and regions previously outlined, by the practical attainment of what must be, from the beginning, the end: a government for the democracy of a united mankind. And just as the region should be the natural extension of the neighbourhood, so the world might serviceably be seen as the natural extension of the region. Indeed, the relationship between region and world might well be based on the relationship between neighbourhood and region. The population ratios would be of a similar order.

Each regional assembly each year, at the conclusion of its term, would elect two of its members from a list of twelve chosen by lot, as delegates to the world assembly. And the world assembly would in turn choose a world directorate, half by lot and half by secret ballot, from among its own members, for a term of three years. This directorate, like its regional counterpart, would be a comparatively small executive sector of an organic parliament;

would have its chairman elected directly by the assembly; and would, by the due combinations of its members, empower a first secretary to appoint executive colleagues and pursue particular policies.

Since the possibilities and dangers of developing a political oligarchy, as the needs for diffusing experience of political authority, would be certainly no less on the level of the world government than on that of the regional, the single term service limit should apply as well to membership of the world assembly and directorate. And since some basic administrative continuity would be required by the world directorate, such safeguards against bureaucratic entrenchment and secrecy of deliberation as have been suggested for the permanent civil service in the regions, should equally inform the employment of a world civil service.

To pursue the regional parallel further: the world directorate would, for two out of every three years, be facing an assembly which had not chosen it; and clashes on policy between the two would sporadically arise. Here, too, such conflict might in the first instance be resolved if the world administration submitted, to amend its programme accordingly; or resigned, leaving the directorate to constitute a new administration, able to command a majority and yet pursue a programme acceptable to the assembly. Should the administration, with the support of a majority in the directorate, remain adamant, however, the two houses would meet together, to reconsider the issue jointly and to prevent an unimportant majority in the assembly from prevailing. If the policy of the administration was, then, rejected again, but still supported by a majority of the directorate, the issue would be referred to the world tribunes:* who could, by a three-quarters majority of their number, impose a solution; or, by a two-thirds majority, dissolve the directorate for new elections; or, in the final event of being themselves unable sufficiently to agree, would automatically resign, for the due selection of new tribunes in their place.

*The referendum, employed to resolve such conflict in the region, would seem too impractical for proper employment on the world level.

The World Tribunes
If regional tribunes should exist – to guard and foster the

freedom of the individual; to supervise political processes; and to arbitrate in disputes between institutions – how much more persuasively must such purposes argue for the existence of world tribunes: as checks on the functioning of what would be ultimate social power, with corresponding dangers of abuse.

These men, three hundred in number, and permitted to serve for only a single term of a single year, would, like their regional counterparts, be selected by lot: but with one third drawn from former first secretaries of regional administrations; one third, from former regional tribunes; and one third, from former neighbourhood tribunes. This composition would allow for the claims of administrative experience; and – given the very large and steadily increasing number of former neighbourhood tribunes – a significantly representative element of the general citizenry.

In addition to the powers they possessed to resolve otherwise intractable disputes within the world parliament, the world tribunes could, by a two-thirds majority, order the due reconstitution of any regional authority. They could, moreover, by a simple majority, set aside the verdict of any court; or, by a two-thirds majority, any decision of the regional tribunes or the inter-regional arbitration panels. By a two-thirds majority vote, they could prevent the application of any new law that they declared to be in conflict with the rights of the person; and by a simple majority, introduce draft laws for approval by the world assembly.*

They themselves would be immune to arrest or prosecution of any kind not only during their term of office, but for two years afterwards. And any decision duly taken by one set of world tribunes could be reversed only by both a three-quarters majority vote of its successor and a two-thirds majority vote of the world assembly that would then be in session.

Means of Enforcement

The possibility of irreconcilable conflict between a region or regions and the world government must not be left, however, for the formal powers and developing popular prestige of the world tribunes to confront alone. And, in any event, provision must be made for the appropriate security and enforcement of

*The issue of direct access to the world tribunes for the individual citizen is subsequently treated in the section dealing with economic government.

world government operations. There would, accordingly, have to be a world police force: in the main, to function at the world level as the regional forces did locally; and ultimately to protect the integrity of mankind against separatist assaults. Yet the risks to the freedom of the individual in the establishment of such a force can scarcely be exaggerated; and its existence would have to be qualified by an abundance of safeguards.

To begin with, the membership should be composed overwhelmingly of ordinary citizens, selected by lot, for a term of one year, from those who had just completed their service in the regional forces. And since a commitment to the unity of the world, in contrast with any regional claim on allegiance, should be promoted for just such occasions of separatist assault, these citizens must be drawn from all the regions together; and not in separate contingents from each region, to produce a sort of federal composition.

The force would, of course, require an administrative command; and it is against the abuse of its purposes by this command, that precautions would need to be taken. The general safeguards of the world civil service would apply: with administrators and their assistants permitted to serve in the police department for no more than two years. But further, particular measures would be advisable.

A special police commission of sixty members would be selected by lot: with half drawn from the list of former regional judges, and half from the list of former world assembly delegates, to serve for an unrepeatable term of eighteen months. This commission would supervise the functioning of the force: with special scrutiny given to the activities of any intelligence section, whose files every commissioner would at any time be entitled to examine. Though a simple majority of its members would be sufficient for all ordinary decisions, any use of arms by the force, short of a duly declared state of emergency, would require a two-thirds majority vote.

A state of emergency itself, such as would be produced by the recalcitrance of a region or regions after all statutory processes had been exhausted, or by significant revolt, would involve a situation with which the police commissioners could not properly deal. It would, by definition, reflect a critical challenge to the whole system of world government, and so demand exceptional measures. Yet, it is plain, no political instrument has in the past more consistently served the purposes of despotism than a state of emergency. It should, therefore, be allowed, as an ultimate resort, only with every practical precaution.

First, it should require the specific request, by a three-quarters majority, of the world directorate; then, it should receive the assent of the world assembly, by a majority of two-thirds; and, finally, the world tribunes, by a majority of three-quarters, would have to approve. But more, any such declared state of emergency would automatically lapse six months after coming into force; and if needed again, would itself again need prosecution of the entire preparatory procedure. Just who would exercise power under the state of emergency, the terms of the declaration would have to determine. But whatever the terms, normal authority could be no more than suspended. It would reassume its powers with the automatic lapse of the emergency; or before, should those placed in control by the declaration, resign their own.

The Constitution

Some such scheme, reaching from the direct democracy of the neighbourhood council to the representative institutions of world government, would seem capable of protecting personal freedom and promoting extensive exploration of social relationships, while providing for the organized unity of mankind. Yet to suggest that it, or any other, should inform a final fundamental law, would be to deny the perpetually experimental role that society should play. The difficulty will always exist of how institutions can function effectively without dominating the people whom they are expected to serve. That is why permanent revolution is the proper pursuit of man. Sometimes freedom will be intolerably sacrificed to security; sometimes security, intolerably to freedom. In the tension between the two lies the failure that is the impulse to further social exploration.

The argument for having no written constitution at all, since whatever it prescribes may confine social experiment, is strong; as is the argument for having a constitution of primary principles which may never be altered, so as to ensure a social basement of freedom and security. In the end, of course, it is neither the presence nor absence of a constitution, fixed or flexible, that matters nearly as much as the developed social temperament itself.

Britain has no written constitution, but, by a reliance on precedent and individual laws, generally upholds those civil rights that represent the values of liberal capitalism. In the Soviet system, there are written constitutions which must stand among the most solicitous of personal freedom and the most protective against the arbitrary exercise of power; but which are honoured, by the nature of authority in the state, far more in the breach than in the observance.

The written constitution of the United States has been in general what the changing complexion and priorities of the social order have chosen to make it: excusing and then prohibiting slavery; first fostering and then assailing the racial segregation that followed. Yet it has, too, in its very recital of rights, encouraged the individual citizen to expect their enjoyment, and to consider himself provocatively deprived in experiencing their denial. On balance, therefore, a written constitution for the creative society might be an advantage: in exciting the person to appraise the claims of security by the claims of freedom; and especially in formulating the very impetus to social experiment.

Such a constitution might well be both fixed and flexible, indeed. Certain clauses, composing a bill of rights, would be invulnerable to alteration or removal by any surge of the popular will, however strong. For instance, the right of the person to the natural term of his life would be absolute, so that capital punishment, or killing in the course of police operations, could never enjoy constitutional sustenance. This does not mean that, with sufficient cause, popular institutions could not, or should not, choose to kill rather than be killed themselves. It is reasonably to be supposed that some men might set out to violate the rights, including the very right to life, of others; and that the circumstances of their challenge would require immediate self-protective measures of force by society. But such measures, exercised only through a declared state of emergency, would remain unconstitutional; and should provoke a subsequent searching reassessment by the citizenry of all its institutions. Thus, the constitution itself would automatically summon, one year after such a state of emergency had come to an end, exhaustive public inquiries – under the ultimate authority of the world tribunes then in office – into the genesis and course of the emergency: with the appropriate consequences for officials whose acts had been unwarranted by the circumstances, or for institutions whose essential functioning would be found to have been originally at fault.*

Fixed constitutional provisions would protect, no less than the right to life, the rights of the individual citizen to free speech and assembly; to impartial trial when accused of an offence; to security of his person and possessions against arbitrary acts; and such others as are now formally familiar in liberal societies.

But, further, the constitution would have no less to protect rights formally denied in liberal societies; and without which the rights proclaimed there must remain a mask or a mockery. It would, for instance, guarantee the supreme claim of mankind to the social allegiance of men; the equal access to social power of the individual citizen; his equal share in the ownership and control of productive property; his equal right, within the limits set by the equal rights of his fellows, to pursue the development of his personality as he chose, while receiving equal means of material support; and the freedom, indeed duty, of social units, within the limits of these principles, to experiment with institutions.

Alongside the fixed provisions, therefore, a second constitutional category would contain clauses relating to the appropriate established social agencies, such as have previously been suggested and described. And the clauses accordingly categorized would be

*A state of emergency could scarcely be declared, of course, on every occasion where the police needed to exercise armed force. And in general, indeed, even such police activities as the arrest of armed criminals or the quelling of local riot could effectively be undertaken without means that risked the taking of life or serious injury to the person. The existing police force in Britain, for instance, still manages to protect an aggressive social order of private property with only rare resort to guns. And it is to be hoped that in a pervasively democratic social system, recourse to armed force by the police would be far rarer; as would the incidents provoking it. Yet circumstances could arise where all other means had failed; where the employment of arms was needed to preclude the risk of even greater injury; but where the challenge was not such as to require the disruption of normal government through a state of emergency. Here, too, then, the unconstitutional taking of life, or any other denial of fixed fundamental rights, by the police – permitted at all only by the due vote of the police commission – would have searchingly to be considered, one year afterwards, by a public enquiry, under the ultimate control of the world tribunes.

subject to any amendment, though only by procedures themselves laid down in the constitution: so as to allow for the fullest social experiment consistent with the rule of law.

Thus, in this system, after a trial period of no less than two years, an experiment in new institutions by a particular neighbourhood could, with the two-thirds majority vote of the local council, and the three-quarters majority vote of the local tribunes, be forwarded to the regional authorities for adoption. The region would, if in accord, be required to undertake a trial period of no less than two years itself; and, on the results, could convey, by the two-thirds majority vote of its assembly and the three-quarters majority vote of its tribunes, its proposals to the world agencies for entrenchment in the constitution. A two-thirds majority of the world assembly and a three-quarters majority vote of the world tribunes would then be sufficient to amend the flexible clauses of the constitution correspondingly.

A Matter of Incentives

This system, or indeed any other based on the need for social experiment and on the equal access of all men to social power, implies the deprofessionalization of politics; and this in turn implies the recognition of political office as just another form of socially productive activity. All men must be politicians. But some, by the demands of the posts that they temporarily hold, must be political officials. Ought they, therefore, to be rewarded differently from other citizens?

Doubtless a competent world tribune, even though his achievement of the office was due to the mere determinations of lot, would be likely to command a measure of public respect, for the particular importance of his functions, that would not be accorded a doctor or computer operator, each of them no less competent in his own way. Yet if this particular measure of respect was all that constituted his differential reward, there is no reason to suppose that it would be anything but socially beneficial. It might well promote the sense of particular responsibility involved, and encourage the man to meet the challenges of his office.

Furthermore, the quality of performance will never be the

F

same for all men engaged in the same activity. One teacher may be competent, while another is additionally talented: and society would be right to distinguish, in degree of respect, the second from the first. Or, to consider a combined difference of activity and quality in performance, a great dramatist would probably enjoy a respect that escaped even the highest political official.

Then, there are certain jobs significantly less congenial than others. It would, of course, be a major objective of the creative society to use machines instead of men for these: or where this could not be done, to make their performance as far as possible a function of citizenship itself, so that every able person carried an equal share of the burden. A few hours spent so each week, would, as well, keep the social outlook of the citizen from being narrowed by the preoccupations of his usual work.* But some such jobs would still have to be done by those especially trained for them. And in the creative society, the men who did these would, surely, be accorded more rather than less public respect in consequence.

None of this should mean, however, that any job would be accorded disrespect. For it would exist because the dynamic relationship between the individual and the community had need of it. And, in the end, the creative society would be one in which the person sought his proper reward in the contribution that he believed himself making to the happiness of mankind, and so to his own happiness as a man.

The existence of different degrees in public respect should be enough for society to encourage some achievements rather than others, while promoting the personal respect that every man should have for every other, if he is to have any real personal respect for himself. Certainly there would be no place in the creative society for material distinctions: which debase the primary impulse of the person to greed; and the person himself, to merchandise.

In the Western Cape wine-producing districts of South Africa, coloured labour has traditionally been paid part of its wages in drink. The white farmers have long claimed in their own defence that their labour would not have it otherwise. And,

*If bureaucrats in Cuba have cut sugar cane, some of them with remarkable efficiency, for a dozen or more working days at a stretch, the limits to human adaptability are distant indeed.

170

to be sure, their cultivated craving is such, that the labourers not seldom supplement their daily drink allowance by spending some of their cash income at the bars. Is it altogether unreasonable to compare the operations and effects of this 'tot' system to the operations and effects of the 'material incentive', which informs so much of advanced industrial culture?

The material incentive in the literal meaning of the phrase, would, of course, be an essential dynamic of the creative society. For to the extent that material goods liberated men equally from physical pressures, they would promote the resources for social experiment. They would be the instrument of personality. But the material incentive, in the accepted meaning of the phrase today, is the antithesis of this. It is the competitively acquisitive appetite for material goods. It offers an inequality of liberation from physical pressures. And it effects the confinement of everyone instead. It turns personality into an instrument. It becomes its own objective and excuse. Indeed, it is like the craving for drink or addictive drugs. What began as a means is increasingly an end, and a self-destructive end, in itself.

Nowhere is this more apparent, predictably, than in the lives of the rich. There, the material incentive is furthest from natural need. Yet it is none the less influential – rather, all the more so – for that. It is no accident that the cry for still greater material incentives is, in societies of liberal capitalism, led by the already rich and the political parties which more openly represent their interests. And the prospect of larger material reward with less onerous personal taxation does often seem to excite, among such men, a greater investment of effort. In short, there may be some of the rich who feel that they have enough money. But they are the exceptions who merely prove the rule: that however much money one has, it is never enough.

Nor is this solely, even primarily, because material goods are their own reward. The folklore of capitalism is full of historical figures, like Henry Ford and John D. Rockefeller, whose personal expenditure was grotesquely out of proportion to their means. In fact, as capitalism has developed, the self-indulgent tycoon of the Vanderbilt variety has become, more than a breach of taste, a dangerous disloyalty to the collective interests of great wealth; and too conspicuous a personal consumption, a brand of the unredeemable parvenu. Rich men continue exerting themselves to grow richer, though they already earn and own much more than they have any intention of spending or may reasonably enjoy.

Money seems to have a life of its own. And it is crucial to establish why. The first answer is that money is material power. If the measure of access to goods is money, then money confers not only possession of such goods, but also, of course, the power involved in choosing what to possess. An absolute monarch does not need to chop off the heads of all his subjects in order to know that he enjoys the supreme power of life or death over others. Indeed, were he to chop off the heads of all his subjects, he would no longer enjoy over others any power at all. And similarly, the material power of money lies at least as much in its suspension as in its use. To buy is an exercise of power. Yet once exercised, the power has been spent: except in so far as what has been bought, may be turned back into money and power again.* The rich, accordingly, never have enough money: because the more money they have, the wider appears the variety of choice, and the greater the impact of decision.

But this is power essentially over the physical environment. Intrinsically connected to it, in societies dominated by competitive material consumption, is social power. This does not necessarily mean direct political power, though such is often enough involved. There are examples in abundance, under liberal capitalism, of those with large financial resources who regard politics as a shady or at least inferior undertaking, and politicians as no more than commission brokers of the system. In Britain and West Germany, Italy and the United States, there are industrialists and bankers who display towards the careerists of government something of the indulgent contempt which the merchants and land-owners of the ancient world held for the specially educated slaves in control of so much state administration.

The social power of money is far more than its material and political capabilities. Money is, simply, what society under capitalism, however liberal, is about: so that social relationships

---

*Which is why, paradoxically, it is the rich, who can so easily afford to buy obsolescent material goods, who are usually so concerned to enjoy and to earn simultaneously, through acquiring such goods as will appreciate in value: while the poor, who cannot afford the commodities of both pleasure and investment, from country houses to impressionist paintings, enjoy only at the cost of spending.

are primarily, when not exclusively, financial ones. This is profoundly apparent, inevitably, in the law.

' "Did you ever take a look into the Penal Code? You have to read as far as page 177 before you come to anything about crimes against human beings. One day later on, when I retire, I'll work it out precisely. But let's say that three-quarters of the Code, if not four-fifths, is concerned with goods and chattels, real estate, forged currency, forgeries of public and private documents, falsification of wills, etc., etc. In short, with money in all its shapes and forms ... To such an extent that Article 274, on mendicancy, comes before Article 295, on wilful homicide. . . ." '[4]

Simenon's Paris detective speaks with the voice of an outrage not specifically Marxist but essentially humanist, at a society of money rather than of people.

Money is personal relationships. Money is, even, personality itself. As Emerson and Thoreau saw, equally with Marx, men and women in such a culture value each other, and so finally themselves, by what they have, rather than by what they are. Their money does not belong to them; they belong to their money. It chooses how they work, and how they play; where and with whom they live; what they talk about and what they think; why they live at all. Money has, indeed, become life. For is life under liberal capitalism, sheerly imaginable without money? There is not a derelict, in the gutters of the contemporary city, who can survive without it. Even those who repudiate the whole culture, in their small revolutionary communes, require it. And the professing socialism of the Soviet system is busily engaged in competing with such bondage by a bondage less and less distinguishable.

The moral horror is stupendous: we do not think about it, as we do not think about the possibilities of nuclear destruction. Only the last remnants of a peasantry within industrial society, or the primitives of agricultural subsistence without, still retain some measure of freedom from the dominance of money. And they do so, in general, less from choice than from necessity.

For there is, to be sure, no escape in a return to agricultural subsistence: in a retreat from the machine. Thoreau's Walden Pond is no answer to the millions of contemporary Boston, let alone the hungry and shelterless squatters of contemporary Calcutta, whose lives can scarcely be further simplified. Rather, if there is to be an escape from the usurpations of money, it must lie in front, not behind; in exploiting, not discarding, the potentialities of the machine.

The prerequisite is, of course, the appropriate moral commitment. For what is certain is that no human instinct compels man to make of money his master. And the creative society would be one essentially directed to making of money his servant.

It is relevant to remark that when a people feels itself unjustly threatened from without, a relative equality of material deprivation and sacrifice is commonly regarded as not only necessary and right, but even as enjoyable* and elevating. Such, as witnessed by both the public mood at the time and the nostalgia of so many in the present, seems to have been the response of most Britons to the doubtful years of the Second World War. Such seems to be the response of most Cubans to the menaces of, and in particular the economic blockade conducted by, the United States.

The Cuban example is an especially arresting one.† For the revolutionary leadership, excited in part by principle and in part by need, has seized the opportunity to reduce the role of money in the system. And it has done so not by making money scarce, but by making it plentiful; while at the same time removing more and more goods and services from the effective operation of money altogether. Food is strictly rationed; and the cost of the rations, well within the competence of the lowest wage. Rent is fixed at some ten per cent of family income; and intended, at least by government pronouncement, soon to become free. Water and electricity and many amusements, from baseball to

*Why do people so often enjoy minor social emergencies, like prolonged electricity failures, at the time; or even major ones in retrospect? Is it not because such situations bring them closer to each other, and give them a sense of personal meaning and belonging: in contrast with the usual social relationships, informed by money?

†The author can, of course, testify only to the conditions he encountered in February–March 1969. Circumstances may seriously have changed. But if they have, this is likely to be because the experiment was not supported by the politics of equal citizenship. As in the Soviet Union and Eastern Europe, the social problems produced by exclusive power sooner or later drive such power properly to look for their solution in the exclusive material incentive. The pertinence of the experiment remains.

theatre, are already free. With consumer goods in the shops rationed or, in the very few lines readily available, so easily within the means of all; and with a black market of little if any significance any longer: excess purchasing power is either spent in the bars, restaurants, soda fountains or holiday hotels, to which access is less a matter of price than of patience in the queue: or meaninglessly saved. True, incomes are not equal: though discrepancies seem generally more moderate than in the Soviet Union and Eastern Europe. But if an electrical engineer may earn twice, or three times, as much as a waiter does, and effectively do no more than hoard the extra money in a bank or government bonds, his higher income is a materially empty gesture of social respect, or the equivalent of a plastic medal.

Where money buys neither superior consumption nor superior security; where it ceases to play a central social role and so to usurp the priority of human relationships, it dwindles into a convenient medium of exchange. Its mystique disappears. It loses all life of its own.

Cuba is, of course, by the standards of Hungary or Czechoslovakia, let alone those of Sweden or the Netherlands, an industrially backward society. Yet why, one may ask, should it be easier to conduct such an experiment from industrial backwardness and so material scarcity, than from advancement and relative abundance? Why, moreover, should it be supposed that human nature, apparently tractable at a time of national emergency, must remain otherwise intractable?

To be sure, not even at normal times in societies dominated by competitive consumption is the material incentive ubiquitously supreme. Many who know themselves able to earn more in commerce and industry, choose careers in nursing and teaching and social work instead. Many others work at uncongenial jobs only for as long as they may earn enough to sustain themselves. Among the young, the trend is notably away from the material incentives of the system: towards employment and leisure that are informed by the different moral measurements and social prestige prevailing within the culture of revolt. Indeed, the force of the conventional material incentive belongs to the approval, the admiration with which a man's superior resources for consumption are socially regarded. Were the very desire for such superiority to be deprived of social respect, and seen rather as a discreditable weakness of character, this material incentive would soon cease to be the natural impulse that apologists of liberal capitalism and the Soviet system would have us accept.

In the creative society, money would be made correspondingly unimportant by the provision of most goods and services free; and with the citizen using it at all only to enjoy an equal margin of arbitrary consumption, for the enjoyment of personal taste. He might spend his allotment to travel widely: or merely to accumulate other possessions. There is nothing inherently destructive about private property. What, but such, are clothes? It becomes destructive to the degree that it constitutes an exclusive social power and represents a superior personal meaning. Laws allowing the inheritance of no more by value than a sentimental amount of this property; the expropriation of all profit from the sale of private goods, so as to prevent their employment for financial ends; the existence of ubiquitous economic security; and, above all, the related depreciation in the appeal of money: such would make the mere accumulation of possessions manifestly irrational. Whether under this system, indeed, anyone would choose so to clutter his life is to be doubted.

Furthermore, there is no reason why the goods provided free by society should fail to offer a large and expanding area of choice. A privately owned concern like Marks & Spencer in Britain is capable of marketing, through a sharp responsiveness to consumer taste and an inventive collaboration with its suppliers, such variety and quality at so low a price, that customers in their millions, and from all income groups, choose to dress and to feed themselves from its shops. Why should the resources of the whole community, given the investment of similar skills, not be able to achieve at least as much? And the particular example is all the more pointed because Marks & Spencer spends virtually nothing on advertising. The frantic promotion of competitive commodities, so wasteful of human talent and productive means, and so corrosive of the natural environment, the culture, the personality, is no more essential to the supply of quality and variety at low cost, than it is, therefore, to the allegiance of the public.

If countries like the Soviet Union seem unable to provide the sort of service that a single privately owned concern in Britain can do, it is not because they eschew private ownership of manufacturing and marketing, or the promotional techniques otherwise so common under liberal capitalism: but because the employment of their resources is qualified by the priorities of a no less exclusive power. In place of the fraudulently free market is the fraudulent socialism of a bureaucratic regime: that functions, at once timidly and arrogantly, only to promote its own interests.

Proposals for Economic Government

It is obvious that in the creative society, those who produced should have a say in the conditions of production: but significantly no more than any other citizen who, as a consumer, directly or indirectly, of the products, was dependent upon such productive processes. All industry would have to be seen as a common enterprise, for which all in society were individually and collectively accountable, to themselves and to each other. Indeed, it is as members of society, neither more nor less, that producers would be entitled to consider and control the conditions of production. For the alternative is a competitive corporatism: a struggle of mutually antagonistic quasi-states as unexperimental and repressive, as impersonal and morally unaccountable, as is the modern state itself. Not only then would producers and consumers necessarily conflict, but producers conflict with each other, as each corporate entity sought its private advantage.

The crux of the answer would lie in making economic and political activity inter-related manifestations of a vigorous democracy: so that manufacturing and marketing were no less subject to popular concern and control than schooling or mass communications.

Certainly only in the operations of such a vigorous democracy would the usual meaning of efficiency be expanded to include social costing; and the moral accountability of every industrial process be accordingly ensured. At present social costing is either secondary or, more commonly, ignored altogether as irrelevant. What industrial management in its senses, under liberal capitalism, considers, in assessing the costs of production, the aesthetic effect of a factory on the landscape; or the long-term impact of waste materials on the yield of surrounding resources

177

like water and air? And the evidence of rapid pollution suggests that bureaucracy in the Soviet system is scarcely more concerned to evaluate material growth by what social shadow it casts.

A citizen body sufficiently involved in sifting the pertinent information and establishing the broad lines of policy would not allow the prospect of more potent pesticides at half the current social cost in labour and raw materials to obscure considerations of cumulative damage that the processes of production or the products themselves might cause to the natural environment. It would balance the lower material costs of airports in areas of high population density against the cost in the discomforts of noise; and might well choose, at the investment of much greater immediate social resources, airports at the coast with rapid land transport to the population centres.

It is this same social costing that would inform technology in steadily stretching the perimeter of the most serviceable unit for advanced industrial production. There would be few, if any, industrial processes that could reasonably be conducted within the independent resources of a single neighbourhood. The number and variety of those that could reasonably be conducted within the independent resources of a region would fast diminish. And it would be possible to arrest, let alone reverse, this momentum only by denying the liberating potential of the machine. As automation was increasingly employed to release mankind for far more productive and pleasant forms of labour, it might well require a community of more and more ultimate consumers to support many of the major material commitments and routes of necessary further research.

Furthermore, social efficiency must extend the unit of economic functioning so as to promote the competition of techniques: the search for how most effectively to employ the productive resources of the creative society in the service of its moral values. For nothing previously proposed should rule out a crucial role for competition of a creative kind in economic processes. The competition of people for private advantage is essentially degrading and destructive. But the competition of techniques for social advantage must confront indifference, complacency, inertia: it challenges experience and excites experiment. Indeed, it is only where the competition of people does not exist, that the competition of techniques is likely to enjoy its proper play, for ultimate social advantage.*

Thus, though a single region might well be able to afford its own textile enterprise, the existence of two competitive textile enterprises, controlled jointly by the inhabitants of two collaborating regions, would excite each to show itself the more efficient, in providing what the public wanted at the least expenditure of human and material resources. Indeed, a dozen regions might decide to expand competition commensurately: though finding in the event that no more than six competing enterprises under joint control were necessary. Experience would continually make new adjustments. And the competition of techniques in production might similarly be promoted in marketing.

Economic Councils

That popular control, beyond the compass of the neighbourhood, would not be direct and immediate, is obvious. The citizens of a region could scarcely be convoked to decide on whether a particular textile design should be adopted; let alone whether a machine required overhauling. In some measure, an economic enterprise would have to be self-governing. Yet, of course, ultimate control may be so ultimate that it ceases effectively to be control altogether. Institutions would have to be developed which enabled necessary decisions to be made at the place of work, without relegating the individual citizen to a solely outside role, as judge of government in its overall aspects.

Each productive or marketing unit, like a factory or store, within a particular regional enterprise, might accordingly be managed by a council that comprised in equal proportion, representatives of the workers themselves; of individual citizens; and of the regional commission for the enterprise. The workers would provide their representatives from among their own number, with half chosen by lot and half by secret ballot; the regional commission would appoint, from among its own

*The scandal of light-bulb manufacturing, with products that would last much longer at little more cost, kept from the market in the interest of company profits, is one of many examples, under liberal capitalism, of how socially beneficial techniques are discouraged or suppressed. And the incidence of deliberate shoddiness in existing products is so vast and well attested as to have made 'planned obsolescence' into a platitude.

179

members, its representatives to the council; and representatives of the general public would be selected by lot from among all citizens in four surrounding neighbourhoods of the work unit. Such a council would normally serve for a year: with membership disqualifying any further service in such a post; and decisions taken by a two-thirds majority of members.

But provision would have to be made for resolving serious conflicts within the council, or between the council and the regional commission. Any decision of the council to which more than one third of its members formally objected, would automatically go to the regional commission for approval or rejection. And in the presumably rare event of a serious conflict between council and commission, the commission might, though only once, order the reconstitution of the council, with new representatives chosen for each of the three elements. In the presumably even rarer event that the new council also rejected the policy of the commission, it might pursue its own, until the constitution of a new commission, whose judgement would then be binding.

Regional Economic Commissions

The regional commission, would, indeed, be the centre of the system. It would co-ordinate the activities of particular workplaces in an integrated enterprise, through its determinations of policy and the membership of its own representatives in work-place councils. It would provide, through its own composition, an inter-play of opinion and purpose among producers, consumers, and overall social authority. And it would promote, through its delegates, inter-regional economic projects.

The membership of such a commission would, accordingly, consist of representatives from the entire work force in the relevant enterprise, chosen by lot without regard to place of work; an equal number of consumer representatives, again chosen by lot, from among all citizens of the region; and an equal number of regional government representatives, appointed by the regional directorate, with half coming from the ranks of the civil service, and half from members of the regional assembly. The commissioners would normally serve for an unrepeatable term of two years; would select, from among their number, representatives to serve on the councils of the constituent factories or stores; and reach decisions by simple majority voting.

Yet, since conflict between a particular commission and the regional directorate might occasionally occur, a standing committee of the regional assembly, selected by lot, would exist for each economic enterprise. This committee, in the event of an appeal from either the regional directorate or the commission against the policy being prosecuted by the other, would attempt to resolve the differences. And if this proved impossible, the committee would have the power to order, though only once, the reconstitution of the commission, with new representatives duly chosen for each of the three elements. Should the new commission then continue to pursue the policy of its predecessor, against the continuing opposition of the directorate, the dispute would automatically be referred to the regional tribunes, whose decision would be binding.

If such provisions seem complex, the complexity is not gratuitous. It is demanded by the need to avoid the development of a self-serving, socially-blinkered bureaucracy in any particular economic enterprise : without allowing the development instead of an all-intrusive, ill-qualified domination by the political executive. The various regional commissions must enjoy a measure of responsibility without which mere prudence would dictate inertia; but they should never be allowed to see themselves as responsible for self-sufficient processes, outside the changing purposes of the whole society.

Authority tends to play safe; to discourage tensions in its domain; to seek the protection of precedent rather than risk the possibility of mistake. The inclination of an economic regional commission such as previously outlined, even with the element of ordinary citizens chosen by lot, might well be to lead the quiet life and keep to techniques that had so far proved satisfactory. The initiative in promoting creative competition might then well be assumed by the council of a particular work unit, or by the regional directorate.

Inter-regional Economic Delegacies

It has already been shown* how regions might collaborate with one another in particular projects under joint control. But

*See pp. 161–2.

given the special government of economic enterprise, the responsible unit of regional authority would here be the economic commission for the enterprise concerned, and not the directorate.

To illustrate: let us assume that the economic commissions for the manufacture of textiles in seven regions decided to collaborate in operating three competitive enterprises. There would be three separate inter-regional delegacies, to exercise the corresponding responsibilities. And to each such delegacy, each participating regional commission would send its representatives, in equal number, to serve for an unrepeatable term of eighteen months. Democratic control would remain with the commissions themselves: which might, in the last resort, withdraw their support from one of the enterprises, or from the inter-regional collaboration altogether.

But in either such event, terms of compensation would have to be arranged. And a special panel of arbitration would exist for every inter-regional delegacy: with members serving for an unrepeatable term of three years; and selected by lot from a list of former regional tribunes and economic commissioners in the participating regions.

World Commissions of Control
Such inter-regional collaboration would not, of course, constitute the limit of extended economic activity. There would obviously be enterprises that required supra-regional organization and control. Natural resources unevenly distributed across the world could not properly be exploited to the advantage of the particular regions where they happened to be concentrated.

The production and distribution of foods, for instance, would have to be centrally administered, as an undertaking of mankind, so that the right of everyone to a free and proper nourishment might be secured. No region should suffer dearth while another enjoyed a glut; provision would have to be made against the caprices of climate; the use of chemicals would have everywhere to be regulated, as would the intensity of cultivation, to prevent the cumulative poisoning or impoverishment of the earth.

Yet to list such functions is to raise at once the risk of a power so immense and so remote that the direct democracy of the neighbourhood might become mere amateur theatricals, performed under licence. Whether the risk developed, however, would depend on the growth of the whole political system; and on the vigour of its root in the neighbourhood. But certainly there would be little future, if much of a present indeed, for the creative society anywhere, outside the organized unity of mankind.

The administration of supra-regional economic enterprises would belong to world commissions of control: each with a chairman appointed by the world directorate, and with members selected in equal numbers by lot from the world assembly; from a list of all former inter-regional economic delegates; and from a list of all with previous service in a regional directorate: for an unrepeatable term of eighteen months. The commission of control would reach decisions by a simple majority of its members, and this decision would stand unless formally challenged by no less than a two-thirds majority vote of the directorate.

In the event of such a challenge, the issue would automatically be referred to the world assembly's standing committee for the relevant enterprise, and this committee would attempt to compose the differences by negotiation and recommendation. Should it fail, however, it would then call for the intervention of the full assembly, which as a last resort could order, though only once during its own term of office, the commission to be duly reconstituted. Should the will of the new commission's majority still conflict with the will, expressed by a two-thirds majority vote of the directorate, then the issue would go to the world tribunes, whose decision would be final and binding.

The economic role of the assembly standing committees for particular enterprises should not, of course, be limited to an occasion of conflict between commission and directorate. They should provide channels of recommendation and complaint, to the directorate and the commissions, from the various regions, through their representatives in the assembly.

But this process would still be necessarily far from the direct citizen expression of the neighbourhood. And even in a population of several billions, provision must exist for some measure of security against supreme institutional power; some appeal from the individual citizen to the independent judgement of his fellow men.

Recourse to the Tribunes

Direct access to the world tribunes, for all who might wish it, would scarcely be feasible. But the world tribunes should be charged with considering a random sample of all direct appeals to their intervention, from individual citizens. And should they judge it proper, they would use their wide powers accordingly.* This ability of theirs to act, on the application of any person anywhere, would, it is to be hoped, discourage government from abusing social power, while encouraging the individual to insist upon his equal rights.

What is being asked, by the cause of the creative society, is that we should deliver ourselves to the possibilities of trust in and love for our fellows, against a record of so much suspicion and indifference and hate. Compared to this, what were the struggles against the supremacy of a single Church; against the privileges of kings and nobles; against slavery; against primitive capitalism; against the imperial idea?

Will hard won industrial equipment not be destroyed by the incompetence and factionalism of such democracy? Will some citizens not intransigently fight against the denial of the right to inequality : even so far as to pull down the economic building on the heads of all? Will not even the poor among the rich rebel against the attempt to eliminate poverty everywhere in mankind?

For those whose minds belong to the past, and who hear the sounds of the jungle always stirring to advance on the clearings of precarious order, the promise of such revolution is plain. The grass will grow over the feet of the skyscrapers, and hunger will reduce society to marauding bands. Chaos will envelop humanity, leaving death and desolation behind. And even for many of those whose view of their fellow men is not so dark, the risk is simply too great for rational acceptance. If the rewards of success excite the imagination, the retributions of failure stupefy it. The very height of refinement that industrial society has reached, suggests that a fall would be very hard indeed. The culture of subsistence, that has enabled peasant society to survive so many

*See p. 164 for what such powers would be.

calamities of climate and conflict, was the prerequisite victim of the industrial victory.*

Yet what is the price of keeping society as it is? For as long as men are engaged to the exclusive material impulse, each separate population will attempt to advance its standards at the cost of others; and within each, those who have more will attempt to secure and increase it at the cost of those who have less. In the United States, the current consummation of liberal capitalism, where human inventiveness constantly scales new heights, and where there exists a measure of material wealth without parallel or precedent, how far are the miseries of which Hobbes wrote three centuries ago?

> 'It may seem strange to some man, that has not well weighed these things; that Nature should thus dissociate, and render men apt to invade, and destroy one another. . . . Let him therefore consider with himselfe, when taking a journey, he armes himselfe, and seeks to go well accompanied; when going to sleep, he locks his dores; when even in his house he locks his chests; and this when he knowes there bee Lawes, and publike Officers, armed, to revenge all injuries shall bee done him; what opinion he has of his fellow subjects, when he rides armed; of his fellow Citizens, when he locks his dores; and of his children, and servants, when he locks his chests.[5]

As population presses over more predatorily, on the resources made available by social inefficiency for competitive private ends, men will increasingly resent the very existence of others. While

---

*Yet, surely, the refinements of industrial culture have not eliminated, but augmented resilience. West German entrepreneurs, like their bureaucratic counterparts across the frontier, proudly proclaim the part played, in the early post-war years, by the accumulated skills and crisis-roused energies of the ordinary working population. Complex chemical and engineering factories were restored largely by the efforts of those who had worked in them before and who now built machines from wreckage and their own ingenuity.

A senior civil servant, in the West German Federal Ministry of the Interior, interviewed by the author in November 1968, pressed the case for worker participation in the private ownership of industry, by citing the experience of a huge chemical concern. This, with a ground capital of four hundred million D-marks, had been some 87 per cent destroyed during the war. The workers themselves had reconstructed the industry, in 1947–52, with a permanent revolving bank credit which had never exceeded forty million D-marks. By 1953 the volume of production had passed a value of eight hundred million D-marks a year; and by 1968 was running at an annual rate of two thousand million.

the rich demand birth control as the remedy for the recalcitrance of the poor, the poor will go on giving life lavishly as an affirmation of their own; till arbitrary power seeks to impose its arbitrary requirements.

And all the time, each human being dying from inadequate feeding and gratuitous disease, each human being wresting no more than survival from unnecessary work, each human being whose mind is bound like the feet of women in old China, is a loss to the total human reserves of talent and energy, a constant draining of the whole human promise. And that, inevitably, so much more of such reserves should be poured out in the insurrections of poverty, and in the efforts of the rich to crush these, makes the reason gape at the cost which the preservation of privilege requires every man to meet.

Indeed, the keeping of things as they are looks far more like enveloping humanity in a chaos, of widespread conflict and death and desolation, than does the risk of revolutionary experiment. Even if the accident or mad deliberation of nuclear war is somehow avoided, what will remain of a world whose natural resources are being so rapidly wasted or poisoned? What measure of moral pollution will not be required, for social adjustment to the measure of the physical?

The call of the creative society is the call for a reinterpretation of man's very nature. Of course, the risks are enormous. But they offer the possibility of a new mankind, using its united capabilities for an age far more creative than that which now searches the skies: an age to search the personality and find the reaches of freedom. There are so many already who see this, and are committing their lives to bring it about. How should their number and their force not increase, as the progress of our old world is increasingly marked by the individual demeaned? Our choice is not between struggle and rest. It is one between struggle and struggle. And is the struggle of trust and love and hope not better than the struggle of fear and hatred and despair?

REFERENCES

Part I

1　Lester Pearson, *Partners in Development*, London and New York 1969
2　Figures from *Time* magazine, New York, 8 June 1970
3　*The Economist*, London, 13 June 1970
4　Patrick Seale and Maureen McConville, *French Revolution 1968*, London 1968, p. 22
5　Patrick Seale and Maureen McConville, ibid., p. 59
6　From a collection of such inscriptions: Claude Tchou, *Les Murs ont la Parole*, Paris 1968
7　Alexander Solzhenitsyn, *The First Circle*, translated from the Russian by Michael Guybon, London and New York 1968, p. 369
8　See the lengthy report in *Le Monde*, Paris, 4 April 1970
9　See for instance the two articles by K. S. Karol, 'Les Crises de la Société Soviétique', *Le Monde*, Paris, 23 and 24 July 1970
10　Article in *Le Monde*, Paris, 24 July 1970
11　Report in *The Economist*, London, 6 July 1968
12　Joan Robinson, *The Cultural Revolution in China*, London and Baltimore 1969, pp. 12–13

Part II

1　John Reed, *Ten Days that Shook the World*, New York 1960, p. 190
2　T. S. Eliot, *The Hollow Men*, London 1925
3　Robin Clarke, *The Science of War and Peace*, London 1971

Part III

1　Walter Bagehot, *The English Constitution*, London 1963, New York 1966
2　Bertrand Russell, *Power*, London and Toronto, 1938, pp. 313–19
3　Harold Laski, *A Grammar of Politics*, fourth edition London and Toronto 1939, pp. 566–71

4   Georges Simenon, *Maigret and the Lazy Burglar,* translated from the French by Daphne Woodward, London 1968, New York 1963, pp. 23–4

5   Thomas Hobbes, *Leviathan,* Everyman's Library, London and New York 1950, p. 65

INDEX